THE SAS HANDBOOK OF
LIVING OFF
THE LAND

THE SAS HANDBOOK OF
LIVING OFF
THE LAND

CHRIS McNAB

Published in 2002 by Silverdale Books
an imprint of Bookmart Ltd
Registered number 2372865
Trading as Bookmart Ltd
Desford Road
Enderby
Leicester LE19 4AD

Reprinted in 2003

A catalogue for this book is available from the British Library.

ISBN 1-85605-659-7

Editorial and design by
Amber Books Ltd
Bradley's Close
74–77 White Lion Street
London N1 9PF

Project Editor: Chris Stone
Designer: Colin Hawes
Illustrations: Tony Randell, Patrick Mulrey

Printed in Italy by Eurolitho S.p.A.

Contents

Introduction

The principles, though not necessarily the techniques, of survival are actually quite straightforward. To survive in any natural environment you need four elements to be present: shelter, fire, food and water.

This book is concerned with the last three of these elements. Living off the land is a challenge which seldom confronts many of us who exist in urbanized, wealthy societies where almost all our food is produced externally and supplied to us via shops, restaurants and supermarkets. Most of us have become totally detached from the basic realities of food production and preparation, and it is these realities which we must reclaim in order to survive in the wild.

Fortunately, the natural world has a well-stocked larder. There are over 300,000 species of plants and more than two million species of animals on the planet. Not all can be eaten by any means, but a sufficient percentage can. It remains for the survivor to identify the edible varieties, collect or hunt them, and prepare them appropriately for eating. A varied diet is also essential, for the human body depends on a complete intake of fats, proteins, carbohydrates, vitamins and minerals for its healthy function.

This book provides the knowledge for living off the land. It details all aspects of survival nutrition, including how to find and treat water, how to hunt, kill and prepare animals for eating, techniques of identifying and cooking plants, making fire and cooking on it, and how to survive in the world's most extreme climates: polar, jungle, desert, and sea. Yet its principles must be bolstered by practice. An edible plant in a book can look very different when it is seen in the wild, crowded by other similar looking growths. Hunting requires a physical dexterity which is only acquired through time spent stalking creatures. Practising living off the land will also teach the other skills of survival by necessity, such as making a shelter or adapting clothing to the environment. As there is always the risk of poisoning from natural foods, be very sure of your actions before gathering or hunting anything – a mistaken identification could result in death.

Learning how to live off nature is a rewarding skill. Its ultimate value, however, is that of keeping you alive when there is nothing to support you except your own wits and endurance. As we never know when such situations may occur, it needs to be practised with all seriousness.

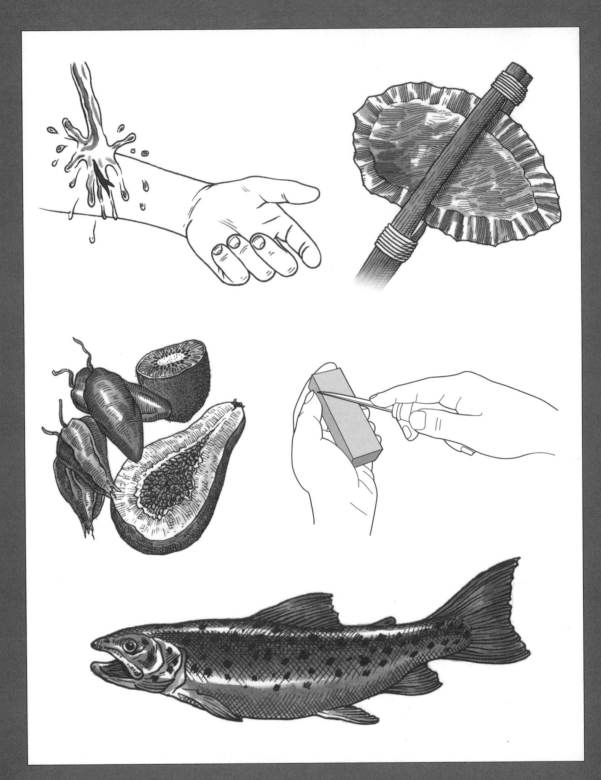

CHAPTER ONE

Basic principles

A survival diet has to be nutritionally balanced if it is to sustain life and health. If the survivor does not eat the right mix of carbohydrates, fats, proteins, vitamins and minerals, it could lead to illness and even death.

It may not be obvious today, but the achievements of the developed world are firmly rooted in agriculture. Without agriculture, there would be no politics, society, governments, arts, business and culture as we know it. Around 10,000 years ago in the Middle East, people began herding sheep and goats as a sustainable source of meat, milk and clothing. The cultivation of single cereal crops also saw a new approach to living off the land. This was the beginning of the agricultural revolution that was eventually to spread across the globe.

Prior to this revolution, there existed the 'hunter-gatherer' societies. The survival of hunter-gatherer societies depended entirely on hunting and killing wild animals and collecting edible wild plants. Gathering food was the main activity of most members of a tribe or group, but even so the diet was uncertain, sporadic and frequently meagre. Population growth was therefore limited by what nature's larder had immediately to offer, particularly in the northern European climes, where winter foods were especially sparse, and the average life-span was only 25–30. Many, in fact, died younger through poor nutrition, and infant mortality probably ran in the region of around 50 per cent.

Agriculture changed everything. Animals reared for meat were domesticated and kept in pens, or on dedicated pasture, to keep them safe from predators. Herd numbers grew steadily. Instead of grubbing around for whatever edible plants they could find, people began to cultivate one or two easily grown crops to provide sustenance. With proper husbandry, single acres of land yield-

Bow and arrow – commercial model

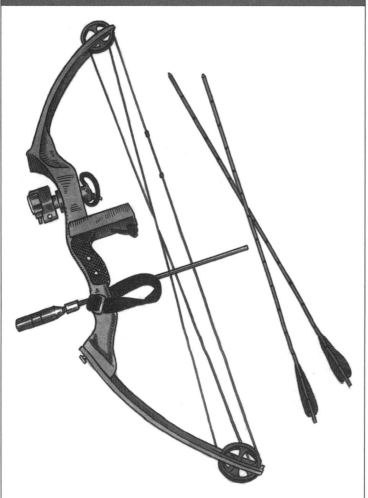

A modern bow and arrow works on the same principles as ancient bows. However, the modern fibreglass or seasoned-wood bow does not lose its tension over time, and is more resistant to the elements. This bow also features a weight bar and a sight, and a pulley tension system which enables the archer to pull over 100lbs (45kg) of release pressure with little effort.

through the efforts of small numbers of dedicated land workers. With organized food production in place, populations rapidly grew and commercial transactions (initially barter) soon followed. And as those who controlled food production inevitably came to wield immense power, politics and government were born.

The developed world has long enjoyed the benefits of the agricultural revolution. In densely populated towns and cities, the superabundance of supplies, coupled with modern, global transportation networks and preservation methods, allows foods to be selected as much for pleasure as for basic survival.

This is clearly an enormous and welcome achievement, but it is not without its disadvantages. In hunter-gatherer societies, the amount of food eaten was, at best, equal to the energy used. In the West, there is ample evidence that people are taking in more food than they burn off. Food with high calorific and fat values is so plentiful, and marketed so persuasively, that obesity and ill-health through overeating have reached epidemic proportions. The World Health Organization estimates that 59 per cent of US males and 49 per cent of US women are clinically obese. An influential US market research company even predicts that the entire US population will be overweight

ed quantities of food that would previously have involved scouring hundreds of acres of wild land.

Thanks to the growth of agriculture, entire communities could now be fed by 2030. In the UK, 50 per cent of all adults are overweight. The cost of treating the serious illnesses and chronic conditions associated with obesity, such as heart disease, strokes, diabetes and certain cancers, puts an enormous burden on healthcare spending.

These figures are grim, but quite apart from the significance of long-term health risks, widespread obesity is a sign that few of those who consume food have, any longer, a direct connection with the means of production or preparation. Take away pre-packaged supermarket products, fast-food chains and restaurants, and a great many people simply would not know how to keep themselves alive. Drop the average city-dweller into the middle of a wilderness, jungle or a desert in just the clothes he stands in, and within a week he would, most likely, be dead.

Fortunately, few of us will be thrust into a genuine survival situation but, thanks to the growth of outdoor adventure sports and long-distance travel by car and plane, it is happening more and more. And unfortunately, our comfortable urban lives don't prepare us to take on a natural environment should things go wrong. This book intends to put that right.

NUTRITION AND SURVIVAL

There are two essential principles to living off the land. First, the food that is gathered and eaten must supply all or most of the body's nutritional requirements in terms of proteins, fats, carbohydrates, vitamins and minerals. An unbalanced diet – one consisting of a limited range of foodstuffs – can actually be worse than not eating at all. A classic example of this is 'rabbit starvation'. Rabbits are an accessible and often plentiful food source in varied terrain. But, though they provide protein, digesting rabbit actually burns up more of the body's vitamins and minerals than its meat supplies. A diet based exclusively on rabbit will eventually strip the body of vital elements and can, ultimately, be fatal.

The second principle is that the energy value of the food eaten should equal the energy expended in activity. When the human body runs out of reserves of fat to supply energy, it then begins to break down muscle and tissue to supply its energy needs. This can lead to death quite rapidly. To prevent this happening, it is important to eat enough food to provide the body's energy needs. If this is simply not possible, then delay the breakdown of body fat reserves as long as possible by limiting physical activity and waiting for rescue.

The body requires five main elements to function healthily: proteins, fats, carbohydrates, vitamins and minerals.

Proteins

Sources of protein are primarily all types of meat and fish, and can also be obtained from milk, eggs, nuts, grains, pulses and even some categories of fungi. There is little to be found in vegetables. Proteins are essentially the building blocks of life. They are made up of amino acids, molecules that are found in most natural life forms. In human beings, amino acids are essential to maintaining tissue health and growth, and the effective functioning of the metabolism. In total, there are about 80 different types of known proteins. Human beings require about 20, 11 of which are obtained from food, while the remaining nine are internally produced (when proteins from food are broken down into amino acids, these acids then create new proteins). Proteins support cell repair and function, and aid the immune system by helping to create antibodies (cells that attack and destroy hostile bacteria or viruses that enter the body). They are also crucial to the formation of muscles and body organs, and assist blood clotting in the event of injury.

This list is by no means exhaustive, but it is clear that protein deficiency is a serious matter. Without adequate supplies of protein, the survivor will experience serious health

Food groups

A diet consisting of the food stuffs shown below would provide all nutritional needs in a survival situation. Nuts (A) are high in fats and proteins, fungi (B) contain several basic minerals and B-group vitamins, fruits (C) are extremely high in vitamins A, B and C, honey (D) contains sugars required for energy, and fish (E) is high in protein.

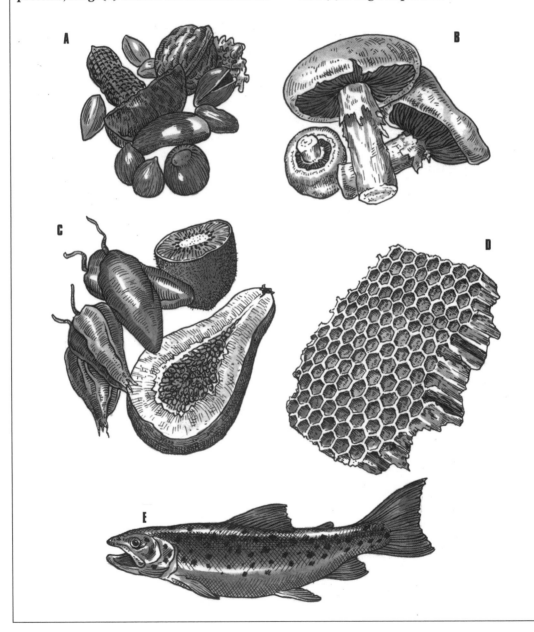

problems, including: a chronic drop in energy levels and mental acuity; the body's ability to heal itself after accidents will be impaired (which is particularly serious in the field, where environmental hygiene is poor); problems with organ function; and susceptibility to illness. Should the body's supply of fats and carbohydrates be used up, all of the above will be exacerbated as the proteins in muscles and organs are broken down.

Fats

Sources of fats include animal foods (particularly red meat and oily fish), oils, eggs, milk and nuts. As fats are indissoluble in water, they place heavy demands for water on the digestive system. Therefore, in a survival situation where there is little water, it is best to avoid fatty foods.

Fats have had a fairly bad press because of their contribution to the West's obesity epidemic. However, fats as a source of energy are cornerstones of human survival. When fats from food enter the body, they are broken down in the blood by special enzymes or stored as reserve deposits. During this breakdown process, heat and energy are released, one reason why they are essential for the survivor. But there are many other reasons. Fats contain cholesterol, a type of lipid (a substance made up of carbon, hydrogen and oxygen) that plays a crucial role in cell repair and function. Fatty layers around the body stop water evaporating too quickly through the skin, which in turn aids heat retention. Also, fats and cholesterol make a general contribution to the efficient functioning of the nervous system by coating nerves with fatty deposits that enhance the transmission of nerve impulses.

Carbohydrates

Carbohydrates are found in fruits, vegetables, rice, cereals, pasta, potatoes and bread.

Carbohydrates are compounds that contain oxygen, carbon and hydrogen. They are produced within plants during the processes of photosynthesis, and they are an important source of energy provision in much of the animal kingdom. Carbohydrates contain various elements that are easily burnt to provide basic short- and medium-term energy needs, and they actually fuel metabolism itself at the cellular level. Carbohydrates break down into two basic forms. First, there are sugars such as fructose, glucose, lactose and sucrose. (Note: carbohydrates, if eaten in large enough quantities, can contribute to fat reserves because of the body's ability to convert excess glucose into fat.) Second, there are elements known as polysaccharides, which include starch and cellulose.

Vitamins and minerals

The human body needs around 13 vitamins and 25 minerals to assist its proper function. Most people will probably be familiar with vitamins A, B (or the vitamin B range), C (also known as ascorbic acid), D, E and K.

Vitamins and minerals are often required in only microscopic amounts, but are crucial to proper cellular function. They activate enzymes (different enzymes, acting in combination, play a vital role in the body in triggering chemical changes) and other vital chemical processes. Vitamins protect against illness by enabling a properly functioning immune system. A healthy, balanced diet – which according to many healthcare experts should be low in fat, sugar and salt and high in fruit and vegetables – will normally provide most of the vitamins and minerals the body needs. (Vitamin D, though, which is present in fish oils and liver, can also be synthesized in the skin through contact with the sun's ultraviolet rays, while niacin is produced in the body from the amino acid tryptophan, and some minerals are formed in the gut by bacteria.) However, doctors in developed societies are starting to see cases of technical malnutrition as a result of unbalanced diets, especially those that rely heavily on an excess of meat and fat, and include little or no fresh fruit and vegetables.

In a survival situation, when foodstuffs are difficult to obtain and reserves of energy low, vitamin and mineral deficiency can be a major problem. To prevent this happening, base a survival diet on equal amounts of meat and plant foods – if at all possible – and avoid reliance on just one type of food, even if it is readily available. Of course, if a rescue is in prospect within 24 hours, then one food source will be fine. But the survivor should always project to a worst-case scenario and, after 24 hours, start planning to gather a wider range of foodstuffs.

BALANCING NUTRITION AND ENERGY

Eating a balanced diet in a survival situation does not call for a lavish spread three times a day. The variety of foods obtainable straight from nature's larder will never match the range or luxury of the supermarket trolley, but it doesn't need to. A few fish a day accompanied by one or two vegetables or fruits will provide protein and fats (in the fish) and carbohydrates (in the fruit and vegetables). Between them, they will provide almost all essential vitamins and minerals.

A survival diet must also meet your energy requirements. Survival is energy intensive by nature, so the survivor must maximize the amount of energy taken in, while at the same time avoiding burning up energy reserves through unnecessary activity.

The energy value of food is measured in calories. A calorie is the amount of heat energy needed to raise the temperature of 1g of water by 1°C. One calorie provides 4.2 joules of energy. Calorie requirements vary tremendously depending on type and level of activity, age and gender (women tend to have smaller daily calorific needs than men). For an average man aged 18–35, an inactive daily routine will use 2500 kilocalories, an active routine, 3000kcals. A day of vigorous physical exertion calls for as many as 5000kcals, lying in bed, 60kcals an hour, and swimming, 720kcals an hour. (N.B. Kcals are a scientific measurement, but in popular terminology 1000 calories are usually referred to as one calorie – the measure used in this book).

Scurvy – the curse of sailors

Historically, the best-documented result of vitamin deficiency is scurvy, which commonly afflicted sailors on long voyages prior to the early 19th century. Scurvy, an illness characterized by loose teeth and bleeding gums, stiff and painful joints, and bleeding under the skin and in the organs, and which can cause death, results from vitamin C deficiency. Because vitamin C plays an important role in the building of collagen in cells, a deficiency leads to poor tissue health. Before the 19th century, ships on long voyages rarely carried any fruit or vegetables – the main sources of vitamin C – because of lack of storage space and because their importance for maintaining good health was not yet understood. Instead, diets consisted largely of salted or dried meats. Scurvy became a massive problem, particularly from the 15th century, when maritime journeys, mainly for trade, became increasingly ambitious in scope. Scottish naval surgeon James Lind finally solved the problem in 1753. Having correctly identified inadequate diet as the cause of the illness, his prescription – that sailors on long journeys should eat oranges, lemons or limes – was instantly effective.

An important factor when determining the calorie intake to activity ratio is the calorific value of food. Take, for example, the following foods, each in 100g (3.5oz) portions.

Food (100g/3.5oz)	Calorific content (kcals/kjoules)
Butter	770/3234
Cheese	350/1470
Milk	66/277
Rice	122/512
Beefsteak (grilled)	300/1260
Sausage (fried)	360/1512
Cod (fried)	140/588
Salmon (steamed)	200/840
Cauliflower (boiled)	10/42
Potatoes (boiled)	80/336
Potatoes (fried)	245/1029
Apple	47/197
Banana	77/323
Raisins (dried)	247/1037
Almonds (shelled)	598/2511
Brazil nuts (shelled)	644/2705
Chocolate	590/2478

In everyday life, foods with a high calorific content should play a limited part in your diet. In a survival situation, they should be maximized. Fried foods undergo a significant calorie boost, and that nuts are probably the best concentrated sources of energy, and should be treasured when found.

Calorific values also determine the types of food that should be taken on survival expeditions or outdoor adventures. Most good adventure sports shops now stock conveniently packaged, nutritious and energy-packed survival foods, often in the form of dehydrated meals to which you simply have to add water. These meals have the added advantage of being light to carry. However, there are several non-processed foods that are just as convenient and durable in survival conditions. Mixed dried fruit and nuts, muesli and oats are nutritious and energy giving, and contain high amounts of roughage to aid proper bowel functioning. Complement these with rice, lentils, dried peas, pulses and beans for protein, fibre and sustained energy. Chocolate and biscuits are good as short-term energy solutions, but do not rely on them. The energy from a chocolate bar is quickly burnt off, leaving you more enervated than before.

It is also vital to conserve energy. The rule of thumb in a survival situation is to avoid any effort that is not absolutely necessary. While resting burns up about 70 calories an hour, walking on normal terrain consumes 180. Of course a survival situation gives you plenty to do but there are several measures to take to avoid wasting energy.

When travelling, avoid, if possible, severe terrain with harsh gradients or a very uneven surface. Try to plan routes that involve only gentle gradients or flat surfaces. Travel or work at night (if safe) or during the coolest parts of the day because the higher the environmental temperature, the more energy required. Follow routes that take you to places where food may well be in abundance. Following watercourses, because fish and plants may be in abundance. Flowing water also tends to lead to human habitation because settlements grow around water supplies in wilderness areas. When not working or travelling, rest, preferably in a lying down position. Despite boredom, resist the temptation to fidget or go off wandering. Stay purposeful at all times. Finally, don't carry any unnecessary loads. Weighty personal items that do not contribute to survival should be shed without regret.

EQUIPMENT AND TRAVEL FOODS

For journeys in the wilderness that are planned, not accidental, there are some indispensable pieces of kit for collecting and processing food. It's worth remembering that an adventure in one type of terrain still requires pieces of kit - such as shelter building, signalling and navigation equipment, clothing, etc - that are specific to all the other survival

Hostile environments of the world

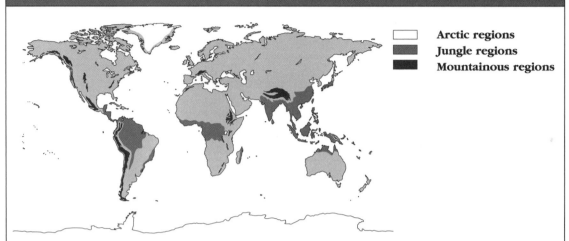

Arctic regions
Jungle regions
Mountainous regions

Natural regions of the world are separated into nine types: polar, tundra, coniferous forest, deciduous forest, scrubland, rainforest, grassland, desert and mountainous. The main determinant of food types in these regions is climate and the availability of fresh water, with humid tropical zones offering the optimum conditions for plant and animal proliferation.

terrain not covered here. Familiarize yourself with these before embarking. It is pointless being able to live off the land only to freeze to death or suffer injury for want of adequate clothing or proper climbing equipment.

A basic survival kit should contain the following items:

Knife
A good knife has multiple survival applications, not least for gathering and preparing food. A Swiss Army knife is useful for its many tools, but it may not be strong enough for the heavy demands of a survival situation. Also, the fact that the blades do not lock in place increases the likelihood of a self-inflicted wound. Take with you a strong, compact sheath knife fitted with a tough antler or hardwood grip, a bevelled, one-sided cutting edge for easy sharpening, and a wide blade back that allows pressure to be applied to the blade itself during difficult cutting tasks.

Water-purification tools
Every kit should contain plentiful supplies of water-purification tablets and, if possible, a water-purifying pump. This excellent device pumps untreated water manually through iodine purifiers into a drinking container, providing instant fresh water. Also take a tin of potassium permanganate crystals – when exposed to water they will purify it.

Water bottle
This should go without saying. Choose your materials wisely; a plastic bottle may be best because it will not split if the water contents freeze, unlike a metal container. However, keep plastic bottles away from fires to stop them melting.

Mess tin
A metal mess tin will make a good cooking pot, but to avoid burns, remember to put a

Sharpening a knife

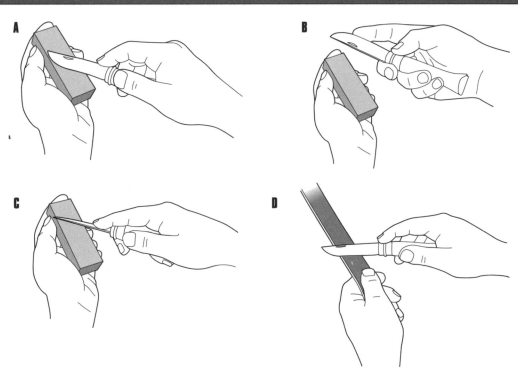

Knowing how to sharpen a knife is not only essential for the efficiency and longevity of the cutting edge, but also for safety. A blunt knife will need more pressure to cut and can slip more easily. The best implements to use for sharpening a blade are a sharpening whetstone and a leather strop.

Wet the stone with water or light oil and stroke the blade across the stone about six times, in a movement away from the body. Then reverse the direction of the blade and stroke it another six times across the stone, this time in a movement towards the body. Keep the angle of the blade

fairly shallow, about 30° from the flat of the stone. Once the blade is sharpened, stroke it backwards and forwards on a leather strop to make the blade edge stronger. Occasionally clean the sharpening stone with a strong soda solution to remove fragments of metal.

cloth around the metal handles before picking it up.

Stove and fuel
Buy a high-quality camping stove, but don't get one with too many fancy features that may get damaged in the field. Take ample supplies of stove fuel and keep it clean (dirty fuel can block your stove fuel inlet) and at a safe distance from campfires.

Cutlery and crockery
Take with you a basic set of plastic crockery: a plate, a bowl and a mug. These will ensure that you don't have to eat direct from scalding hot cooking pots. A set of cut-

Improvized cooking tools

A basic cooking pot (top) can be made out of any tin can. Puncture the rim of the can in three places and thread the holes with string. The can is then suspended over a fire as a boiling vessel. Alternatively, a simple mess tin attached to a forked twig can provide a boiling and frying surface. Avoid using coniferous green woods which have a flammable resin content.

lery will also allow you to eat quickly and hygienically.

Waterproof matches

Waterproof matches are coated in wax to repel water. Still, they're best kept in a watertight container for protection. You can also make waterproof matches simply by dipping match heads into the liquid wax of a candle and allowing them to dry. When the matches are needed, peel the wax away using a fingernail.

Safety pins

Take a selection of various sizes, as these can make improvised fishhooks.

Fishing equipment

A basic survival fishing kit should consist of two weights of line, fishing hooks, floats, splitshot and possibly one or two lures. Keep all fishing tackle together in a dedicated tin.

Wire saw

As well as being indispensable for building shelters, a wire saw is useful for butchering large animals. Coat with a thin layer of grease and keep in a sealed plastic bag to prevent rusting.

Thin wire

A long section of thin, flexible wire has many uses, not least in building snares to catch animals.

The above list is not exhaustive but in a potential survival situation these items will significantly improve your chances of successfully gathering and processing natural foods.

Of course, the fact is that many survival situations are unplanned. In the event of being stranded unexpectedly in a mountainous region after a plane crash, it is unlikely that a survivor will suddenly start pulling out lots of survival equipment. (You should perhaps get into the habit of carrying a small survival tin with you – a tobacco tin is ideal as it is large enough to contain many of the items listed above.) Fortunately, some tools can be improvised from natural materials, and these can give you a vital head start when gathering food and preparing a shelter. Stones provide some of your best materials. Break a lump of flint in two by smashing it over a rock and it will leave some very sharp edges that can be used for cutting wood and shattering bone. Slivers of the flint tied to a handle can also make good 'knives' for preparing meat, fish and vegetables.

Contents of a survival kit

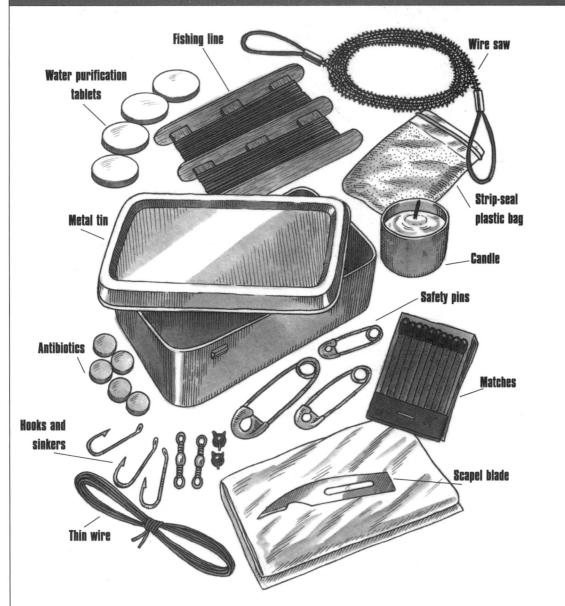

Fishing line

Wire saw

Water purification tablets

Strip-seal plastic bag

Metal tin

Candle

Safety pins

Antibiotics

Matches

Hooks and sinkers

Scapel blade

Thin wire

In the wilderness the survivor's kit is his or her only lifeline, so the diligent maintenance of a survival kit is vital. Metal objects should be coated in a light film of lubricant to prevent rusting, tablets and matches should be stored in a watertight plastic bag, and wire and fishing line must always be wound up carefully after use, free from knots.

Making a stone axe

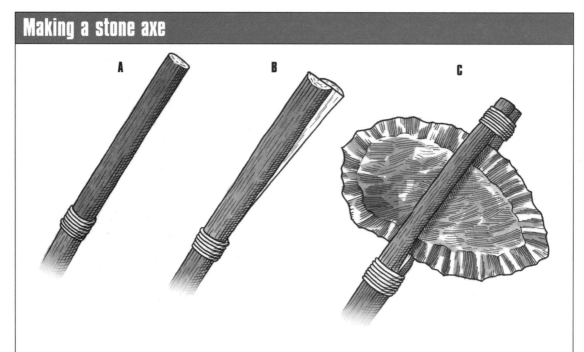

A   B   C

Constructing a stone axe in three easy stages. String is knotted tightly around the shaft of the axe about 9in (23cm) from the end (A). The wood is split down the centre to the tied section – the tension of the string prevents the wood from splitting further (B). The axe head is inserted into the split and secured by tying the forked end firmly together (C).

A slightly more complicated but worthwhile tool is a basic stone axe. To make one, take a hand-sized flat stone and gradually scrape and chip a cutting edge around the entire circumference by working from both sides of the stone with other (softer) stones, pieces of antler or hard wood. Working from a piece of split rock is even better, as the facet of the split naturally lends itself to sharpening. Once the stone is sharpened, it can be set into a piece of wood that forms a handle. Do this by taking a long, thick, hardwood branch. Tie a piece of cord very tightly around the wood about 9in (23cm) from one end and then split the wood from the nearest tip down to the tied point. Insert the axe head into the split and then bind the wood very firmly with twine just above the stone to hold the axe head in place. This axe is very good for basic chopping, but it will not be strong enough for heavy-duty use, and a dislodged axe head can be lethal.

Another useful improvised tool is a bone saw. This is one of the many implements easily made from animal bones. Small bones and ribs can be sharpened into needles, pins and even stabbing weapons, while flat bones are sharpened along one edge to serve as scrapers. The bone saw is usually made from large shoulder blades. Split the bone in half, and then along the split fashion saw teeth using your knife. The resulting saw will be useful if you have to butcher large animals.

HEALTH AND HYGIENE

It is ironic that, in developed nations, nature is generally marketed as a very benign force. 'Organic' foods are generally understood to be healthy and wholesome. Cosmetics are marketed on the strength of their 'pure, natural' ingredients, while mineral waters are promoted as aqua vitae that restore health and wellbeing. There are, of course, genuine grounds for seeing 'natural' products as healthy, especially by comparison with so many processed foods and products, but nature can also be frightening, hostile and dangerous. The survivor must appreciate this duality as he ventures into nature's backyard.

Hygiene is of paramount importance for the survivor. The immune systems of indigenous peoples, such as tribal hunter-gatherers in Borneo and Aborigines in Australia, are conditioned by heredity and environment to resist bacteria and infections that can prove fatal to outsiders. To compensate for this physical vulnerability, obey the following rules of camp-craft and hygiene:

● Build a latrine away from sleeping and eating quarters, positioned downwind. This can simply be a hole in the ground. Each deposit should be covered over with a sprinkling of earth. Always wash your hands after going to the toilet, as parasites are attracted by excrement. Many can be transferred inadvertently from the fingers to the mouth, eventually finding their way into someone's stomach to hatch eggs and grow.

● All water must be purified and all meats must be thoroughly cooked. As in a domestic situation, make sure that raw meats do not come into contact with cooked meats or vegetables.

Making a bone saw

The bone saw is constructed by etching saw teeth into the split edge of a large animal's shoulder blade. While unsuitable for cutting resilient hardwoods, the saw can be used for butchering sizeable animal kills. Large jawbones are also suitable for converting into saws, while detached teeth can be set in wood as another saw type.

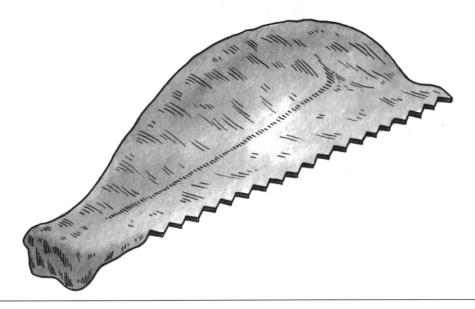

Selection of travel foods

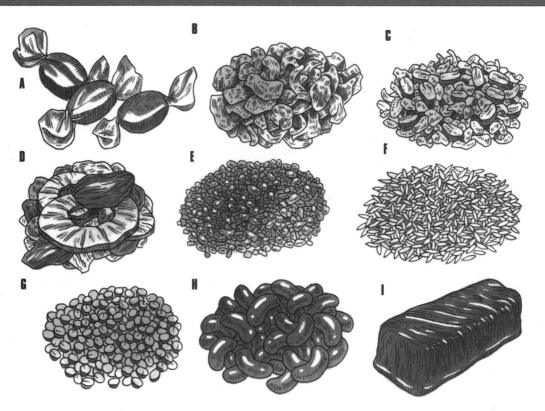

Pre-purchased foods, which are a good idea to have in your supplies in all survival situations, should be light in weight, compact, have a high nutritional or calorific content, and a long shelf life. The following are good examples: boiled sweets (A), trail mix (B), museli or granola (C), dried fruit (D), oats (E), rice (F), lentils (G), kidney beans (H), chocolate bar (I).

- Make a dedicated storage area for food-stuffs in the shelter. Keep food away from the campfire (unless it is being dried or smoked) and away from wild animals.
- Wash your hands and wrists before eating. Try to do this with purified water if possible, as a river or stream may actually contain the parasites or disease-bearing parasites that you are trying to avoid.
- Dental health is important. Improvise a toothbrush by chewing the end of a short soft-wood stick (make sure it is a non-poisonous variety first), which can be used to scrub the teeth gently after eating.
- Isolate anyone who is ill. This may sound cruel, but it is vital, particularly if the person is suffering from an illness with symptoms of diarrhoea and vomiting which may be contagious. Handle the person as little as possible, and wash after doing so. Try to remove any vomit or excrement to a safe distance from the camp, and bury it in a fairly deep hole or burn it.

The fact remains, however, that for the survivor unaccustomed to natural environments, illness is a real possibility. Listing the types of illness that potentially lie in wait across the world would fill an enormous medical textbook, but there is one particular condition of particular relevance to this book – poisoning. When living directly off the land, there is a very real chance of eating or touching something poisonous. This is especially true in jungle or woodland environments, where there are hundreds, even thousands, of different species of plants and animals – many, in fact, that would test the identification skills of even a highly trained botanist.

The two most common types of poisoning are ingestion poisoning and contact poisoning. Ingestion poisoning is usually the worst of the two. Symptoms of ingestion poisoning vary tremendously, depending on the substance taken. Those to watch out for are: severe stomach or throat pains; reddening of the lips and mouth; vomiting and/or diarrhoea; difficulty in breathing; and disorientation and lapses in consciousness. Try to ascertain exactly what caused the reaction and even if you can't positively identify it by name, keep a sample in a sealed plastic bag to give to medical staff when you reach help (which should be your objective).

Your first task is deciding whether or not to induce vomiting, if it hasn't already occurred. Vomiting evacuates the stomach of its poisonous contents, but is usually avoided if professional medical help is on hand. A trained medic will be make a more accurate diagnosis and prescribe the appropriate treatment, if it's available. However, in a wilderness setting, the poison should generally be got out of the system as soon as possible, preferably within only a few minutes of ingestion (though it can be done several hours later). Do not induce vomiting if the poisonous substance swallowed is caustic, corrosive or petrochemical as this will only burn the throat on the way back up and may cause asphyxiation. For other plant, food or medical ingestion, make the person vomit by inserting a finger down the throat or with one or two tablespoons of syrup of ipecac and two cups of water. The latter treatment

Treating an animal or snake bite

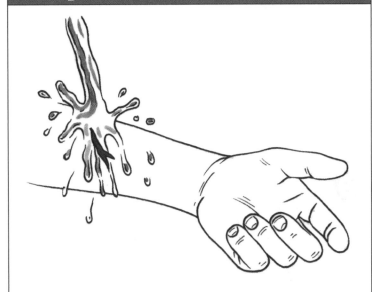

There are two things to consider when treating a bite; stop any bleeding and prevent infection from developing. Bleeding is controlled by placing a thick pad of clean material over the wound and applying firm pressure until the bleeding ceases. Then wash the wound thoroughly with clean water, and apply available antiseptic medicines and bandage a pad of clean material over the wound site. Change the dressing frequently.

Techniques of cardiac massage

The hands must be placed in the right location to deliver cardiac massage. First trace the fingers under one of the casualty's lowest ribs to the point where it meets the breastbone (A). Then mark two fingers' width below this point (A). The heel of the hand which will deliver the compressions sits here.

Note the posture adopted for delivering the compressions. The first aider positions her shoulders almost directly over the point of compression, which allows her body weight to contribute to the force of the push (B).

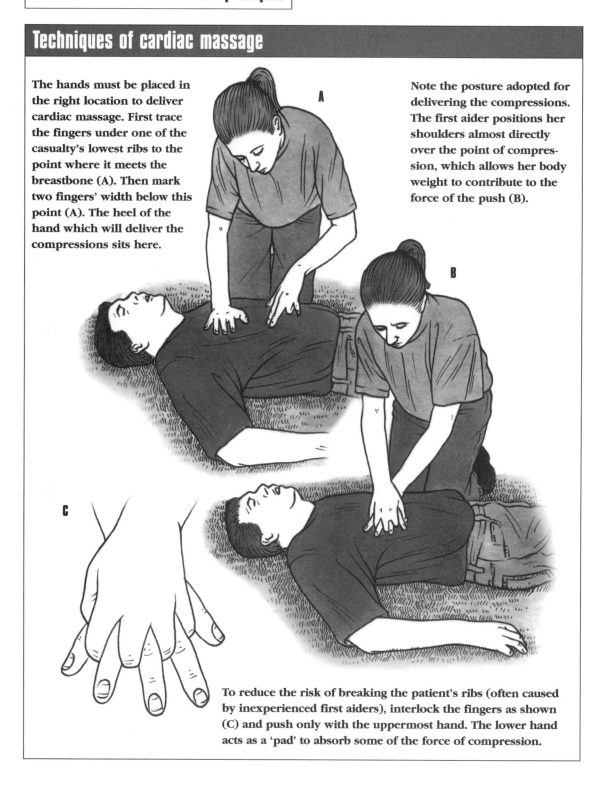

To reduce the risk of breaking the patient's ribs (often caused by inexperienced first aiders), interlock the fingers as shown (C) and push only with the uppermost hand. The lower hand acts as a 'pad' to absorb some of the force of compression.

Resuscitation

Poisons taken by ingestion or contact can lead to respiratory and cardiac failure. With contact poisons, this occurs mainly because of a severe allergic reaction known as anaphylactic shock. Whatever the case, it is useful for to understand when and how to perform artificial respiration and cardiac massage. If the victim is unconscious, kneel close up to the head and place you cheek near to the victim's mouth while looking at the chest. If you cannot feel any breath on your cheek or see the chest move, the person has suffered respiratory failure. To restore the casualty's oxygen supply, first check the mouth for any obstacles lodged in the airway, especially the tongue. Remove any obstacle or pull the tongue forward. Then, place two fingers under the chin and lift it upwards (this lifts the tongue from the back of the throat). Place your mouth around the casualty's, completely enclosing it, pinch the nose tight and blow into the mouth. (Note: in the case of ingestion poisoning, place a piece of material around the rim of the victim's mouth so that your mouth does not come into direct contact with any remnants of poison.) As you do this, the chest should rise, and when you stop, it should fall. Keep repeating until the person begins to breathe on his own, or until professional help arrives. If after an hour the person is not breathing for himself, consider stopping.

Breathing failure is usually accompanied by cardiac failure and vice versa. To detect a stopped heart, place your fingers in the grooves of the neck between the neck muscle and the windpipe, just beneath the jaw. You should detect a pulse there. If there is no pulse, kneel by the side of the casualty and place the heel of one hand about two fingers' width above the point where the lowest ribs meet the breastbone. Place the other hand over the top of the contact hand and then lean over the casualty with arms straight. Deliver a sharp push down, depressing the chest about 1.5–2in (4–5cm), then release. Repeat at a rate of about 100 a minute, or mix with artificial respiration at three breaths, followed by 15 chest compressions. Keep checking the pulse to see if heartbeat is restored. If there is no success after 30 minutes, consider giving up.

should bring up the stomach contents after about 15–20 minutes. After vomiting, wash the casualty's lips and face.

Once vomiting has taken place, attempt to neutralize the remaining poison by absorption. Give the patient either a mixture of tea, charcoal and milk of magnesia mixed in equal parts, or just 1–2 ounces (25–50 grams) of activated charcoal mixed with water. These concoctions have the effect of absorbing the poison into a solid, which later passes out in the faeces as normal.

Treating contact poisoning (i.e. poisoning through touch) is somewhat simpler. Indications of contact poisoning include: a bright red rash; violent itching at the site of contact; formation of blisters; and even systemic symptoms of illness like ingestion poisoning. The affected area should be washed thoroughly with plenty of water to clean away as much of the poison as possible. Make sure the water flows off the body by the shortest route and does not carry the poison to other parts. Then cover the area with a light bandage to avoid contact with further irritants. Wash or remove any clothing that may be contaminated to prevent repeated infection. Take care to avoid coming into contact with the poison while administering the treatment.

CHAPTER TWO

Finding water

Access to drinking water is one of the most important factors in survival, and always takes priority over finding food. Human beings can survive for several weeks without food, but without water they will be lucky to live for a few days.

In any survival situation, the need to find water is paramount. It is even more critical than food. People have been known to survive for three weeks or more with scarcely any food, but not without water.

People who are slightly overweight can often survive longer because of their fat reserves. Women also have a slight endurance advantage over men because their bodies are more geared to storing fat, a product of their childbearing role.

But regardless of level of fitness, gender or personal grit, no one will live longer than an average three to five days without water. In certain environments – the desert being the obvious one – if water isn't found quickly, then a person might not even last a day.

Water is vital to survival because human beings are actually made up of 75 per cent water, right down to the cellular level. Water plays a crucial role in many of the body's natural processes. It helps the kidneys to flush out toxins and body waste, and aids the conduction of nerve impulses in the brain. It is also important for food digestion and in regulating blood pressure. If fluid levels in the body are low, blood becomes thicker and more viscous, which causes a lowering of blood pressure. If blood pressure drops too low, blood oxygenation is affected and the body goes into circulatory shock, a potentially fatal condition.

Unfortunately, the human body is not capable of storing water. In fact, it loses water constantly. A person of average build will lose about 4-6US pints/3.5-5.2UK pints (2-3 litres) of body fluids each day through breathing, sweating and urination. Even a

A rain collecting system

A basic rain collector is made by suspending a large sheet of material between four stakes set in the ground. Rocks placed in an off-centre position create a channel for the rainwater to run down, and the run-off is caught in a bucket. Alternatively, if the sheet is waterproof it can be placed in a hollow on the ground to act as a reservoir.

body at rest in a cool room, breathing slowly and gently, will still lose about 2US pints/1.8UK pints (1 litre). It is impossible to stop water loss so, to compensate, we need to replace lost fluids by drinking. In temperate climates, a body subjected to only moderate amounts of exertion requires at least 6US pints/5.2UK pints (3 litres) per day. This increases sharply in hotter climates and with greater exertion. In hot desert regions, where people work only during the cooler hours of the day, the daily requirement is approximately 10US pints/8.8UK pints (5 litres). A similar amount will be necessary for anyone spending most of the day engaged in strenuous physical exercise in a temperate climate. Water loss is exacerbated by vomiting and diarrhoea, which is why dysentery is such a killer in the developing world.

At all costs, avoid dehydration, which can kill in a very short period of time. A loss of only 1–5 per cent of body fluid will result in thirst, confusion, feelings of aggression, loss of appetite, nausea, chronic fatigue and a racing pulse. A 6-10 per cent loss produces headaches, severe dizziness, inability to walk properly, slurred speech, laboured breathing, dry mouth, shaking and tingling limbs, and blurred vision. An 11-12 per cent loss is potentially fatal. By this stage delirium and deafness set in, plus extreme visual disorientation, commonly described as looking through a swirling blackness. The tongue swells and hardens, it becomes impossible to swallow and the skin shrivels and loses its elasticity. If the condition is not reversed at this stage, death will follow shortly.

REDUCING WATER LOSS

Though water loss cannot be stopped, the rate at which it is depleted can be controlled to a significant degree by modifying patterns of movement, food intake and routine. And, of course, the more water you retain, the less you need to find to survive.

The first principle is: don't engage in any unnecessary physical activity. This is more difficult than it sounds. This calls for a rigorous and conscious attempt to keep all movements and exertions to an absolute minimum. This is hard in a survival situation, as you will probably be working solidly to erect shelters, travelling towards likely rescue, etc. Restrict physical activity to the cooler early mornings, late afternoons or, if the moon is bright, night. When you walk or run, do so in a loping action, with your arms loose by your sides and feet moving in a low, sliding action – this is the most energy-efficient technique. When not directly taking part in an activity, lie down and rest – a worthwhile lesson from the animal kingdom. Most mammals rise in the morning, collect food, eat and then sleep for much of the rest of the day. Follow this pattern as much as possible, and be sure to rest immediately after eating. The body has to work hard to digest the meal you've just eaten. Keep out of hot sunlight and stay cool in the shade (make some shade if necessary). Also, avoid sitting directly on hot ground – put some insulation between you and the earth. Don't smoke or drink alcohol, because both will actually accelerate water loss.

Be very careful how much you eat, because digestion uses water. As water is more important than food, don't eat at all if you only have 1US pint/0.8UKpints (0.5 litres) of water per day. As fat is indissoluble in water and requires a lot of fluid to break it down, the worst possible foods to eat are very fatty foods. Finally, limit the amount of time you keep your mouth open. Every breath out expels small amounts of water vapour. This amount increases when breathing through the mouth, so in a survival situation keep your mouth shut and resist the temptation to talk with colleagues about anything other than essential survival issues. By following these measures, water loss can be kept to a manageable minimum.

SOURCES OF WATER

Water is to be found in surprisingly varied locations throughout the natural world. To understand where and why, it helps to have a basic grasp of how the earth's water cycle – or evapotranspiration – actually works.

The water cycle begins with the evaporation of water into the air. It comes mostly from the world's seas and oceans, which cover 70 per cent of the earth's surface, but also from plants during the process of photosynthesis. As water evaporates and rises, the air becomes saturated with vapour and clouds form. When the air becomes too saturated to hold the weight of the water, the clouds start to release the vapour in the form of precipitation – rain, hail, sleet or snow. This precipitation falls into the seas and oceans and onto the land. From the land, it is either channelled into rivers and streams – which flow back into the seas, lakes and oceans – or soaks into the ground wherever,

Making a bark container

Green bark is both waterproof and flexible, and can be used to make containers for storing water and food. Cut a large rectangular piece of bark from a suitable tree – birch trees are excellent. Soak the corners of the bark in water to give them flexibility, and then gently fold up the sides of the bark to make a 2–3in (5–8cm) high lip around the edge. What was the surface of the tree should be on the outside. Use resin, from the birch tree or the pine tree to glue the sides of the container together. They can be held together while drying by using partly split sticks in the manner of clothes pegs. Once the container is holding its shape, paint or rub pine resin all over the inside to waterproof it.

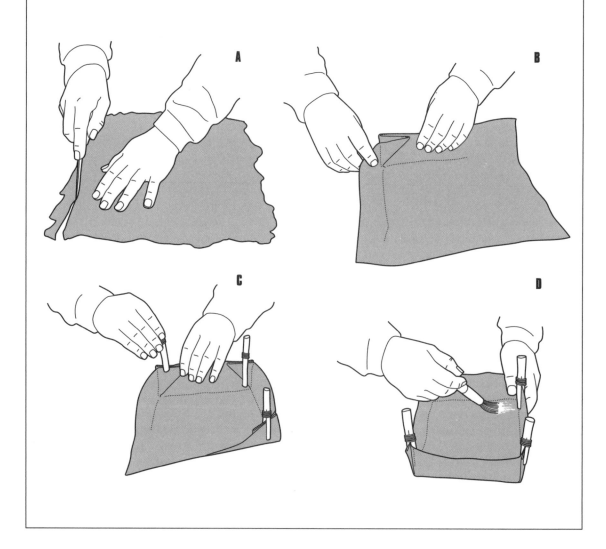

that is, it is not obstructed by natural formations or man-made objects. Underground water is held in the soil, usually in a saturated layer at a specific depth below the surface. The surface of this saturated layer is known as the water table. Underground water also soaks into permeable rocks, or is channelled into underground reservoirs and streams, though these are usually too deep below the surface to be of much use for survival purposes. Once rain returns to open water, and underground water is sucked up into plants, the water cycle begins again.

For survivors, sources of water include: open water (lakes, rivers, streams, snow and ice, and the sea), falling water (rain, snow and hail), underground water (springs), condensation and water from plants. The four main indicators that these sources are nearby are: geological features, plants, animals and the weather.

Geological indicators

Understanding how water relates to the landscape is useful knowledge for the survivor. Travel decisions will be more judicious if the survivor plans his journey around landscape features which promise sources of water. One of the key principles is understanding the relationship between water, high ground and the sea. A mountain range causes moisture-heavy air from the sea to rise up its slopes to form clouds and fall onto the sea-facing slope as rain. So the sea-facing slope is often an abundant source of water, while the opposite side of the range can be surprisingly barren, the clouds having shed all their water before reaching the summit.

Once rain has fallen on the slopes, it seeks out channels in the rock to begin its journey back down to level earth. This is also true of the run-offs that issue from snow-capped or glacial heights. Avoid the high-altitude source of these watercourses, and instead aim to find them at convenient altitudes further down the mountainside. Look for deep cuts in the rock that widen from top to bottom, as these indicate well-carved water routes. These routes will often have shingle or mud deposits clinging to their edges. Also, study the rock for water-collection points, such as natural basins or concave ledges.

Where the mountains or hills flatten out, steady streams and rivers are formed, and lakes are produced. In temperate zones, water is usually fairly prevalent in flatlands. Look for irrigation ditches between fields, or naturally formed gullies and culverts (an underground channel carrying water across a road). Finding fresh water in sandy environments, such as beaches or deserts, is more difficult. The key is to look for low points in the ground where water has been present. In a desert, the trough between two sand dunes can yield underground water, as can the outside bend of a dry river and the point just above the high tide mark on a beach.

Foliage indicators

Because plants are so dependent upon water, their presence is a strong indicator of sources of water. Certain plants are predictive of rain, which allows the survivor to make preparations for collecting rainwater. It is, for instance, genuinely possible to tell the weather by pine cones, which open up when there is moisture is the air, indicating coming rain, and close in fine weather. Plants releasing earthy, musty odours is an indication that rain is in the offing – this is because their spores open in preparation for the downpour.

Plants are also very important locators of actual stored or running water. Fresh green vegetation is a definite sign that water is near, at least in the soil. Where plants suggest underground water sources, explore around those that aren't too high (a little above your own body height), because they suggest a water table at a fairly shallow depth. Fully grown trees, on the whole, don't hold out much hope because their roots can be 15ft (4.5m) deep or more. It's highly unlikely you'll be able to dig down that far.

Of course, plants themselves can be water bearing. Several species of flower have cup-like flowers that hold rainwater, and most plants emit quantities of water vapour, which can be caught by using the transpiration bag method detailed below. Check also the fork of trees, as these sometimes have hollows that collect rainwater.

Animal indicators

The behaviour of wild animals can also lead to water. Like plants, animals are sensitive to barometric pressure. When rain is on the way, herding animals usually move to lower ground to gather together and lie down. However, they can start to do so up to two days before the rain arrives. Other rain indicators are insect-eating birds feeding at lower levels than usual, and squirrels, rabbits and hares engaging in more intensive food-gathering activities.

Following grazing animals can also lead to open water sources (carnivores get a lot of water from their prey so their drinking patterns are unpredictable). Grazers tend to drink at dusk and dawn, so observe their patterns carefully at these times. It is common to find their tracks converging towards a single point, which will usually be a watering place.

Birds can also lead to water, but a bit more caution is required in interpreting their patterns. Don't rely on water birds or birds of prey for help. Water birds can travel large distances to reach water, and, as with animals, birds of prey obtain much of their water from their kill. However, grain-eating birds such as pigeons and finches are useful because their flying pattern will indicate whether or not they are heading towards water. At dawn and dusk, they tend to fly straight and low to the water source. On the return journey, their flight pattern is more sporadic; they rest frequently and fly from tree to tree.

Insects are perhaps the most useful of all when it comes to finding water. Flies tend to stay very close to water, usually no more than 328ft (100m) away. The closer you get to water, the more flies you will notice. The same is true of mosquitoes. Bees require a water supply within approximately 3 miles (5km) of their hive. Once they leave the hive, follow their direction of flight. But perhaps the best water indicator of all in the insect world is the ant. Ants usually march towards water in a regimented column, and if you see them moving up a tree this way, they will almost certainly be heading for a water reservoir in the trunk.

Weather indicators

'Weather indicators' don't so much tell you where water is, but when it will come. The most useful guides in this regard are wind and clouds.

Clouds are an unmistakable sign of the weather to come, whether good or bad. And the clouds that predict rain are naturally of greatest interest to the survivor. When such clouds are spotted, the survivor can either make preparations for catching rainwater or head towards the part of the landscape where it is raining. The clouds to look out for are:

Cumulonimbus

These large, dark and low clouds form impressive towering shapes, sometimes stretching up more than 20,000ft (6000m) in height. Cumulonimbus clouds signal rain, hail and wind. Massive anvil-shaped cumulonimbus suggest that severe storms are impending.

Cumulus

Cumulus clouds are those large, dreamy, white and fluffy clouds usually associated with fine days. However, if they gather together and darken, then rain is to be expected.

Cirrostratus

These are thin, high-altitude clouds made mostly of ice-particles. They are often described as looking like white threads or veins. One of their distinctive features is that they make a pale or lightly coloured halo around the sun and the moon. If the halo gets bigger, then dry weather is on the way; if it contracts, expect rain.

Nimbostratus

Nimbostratus forms a dark, low-level covering of cloud that dims the light. They usually indicate approaching rain or snow within approximately six hours, a precipitation that is likely to be heavy when it does arrive.

Stratus

These are very low-level grey clouds that scud the tops of hills, giving the impression of a ceiling of fog. They are usually accompanied by light drizzle, but if the wind picks up, then heavy rain is on the way.

In a survival situation, identifying which of these clouds are in the sky can be of use in finding water. However, some of these clouds can foretell particularly severe weather conditions that can bring dangers such as exposure, mudslide, lightning and

Making a water carrying frame

Carrying a large container of water over distance is made far easier with a carrying frame. To make one, first cut a Y-shaped bough from a tree, leaving about 1ft (30cm) in length beneath the fork and about 3ft (1m) above it. The distance between the tips of the forked branches should be just greater than shoulder width. Make some notches in the ends of the three arms of the frame, about 3–4in (8–10cm) in from the tips. Tie string or cord around the notches on the two forked arms of the 'Y', then bring the strings down to tie around the base notch of the frame. This effectively creates shoulder straps. Tie your water container to the frame on the side opposite the straps, and hoist the frame onto your shoulders like a ruck-sack. If the straps cut into your shoulders, wrap pads of material around them to protect them.

blizzard. Don't build rain-collecting devices during a heavy downpour. Take shelter instead, and, after it has passed, collect the plentiful supplies of water that remain.

Clouds are not the only indicators that rain is on the way. Here are some other useful signs that rain is heading your way:
- A grey and overcast morning usually means rain later.

- A misty morning means rain in the afternoon if the mist has not lifted by midday.
- Sound carries further just before rain as noise transmits itself more efficiently through the moisture-soaked air.
- Curly hair tends to get tighter and more unmanageable before a downpour.
- Arthritis sufferers complain of increased

Signs of a poisonous water supply

The water area shown below features several indicators that it may be unsuitable to drink. The water is stagnant, suggested by the profusion of cattails and rushes and the lack of water flow. The foam and persistent bubbles on the surface are the result of decomposition taking place and releasing bacteria within the water, but could also suggest chemical pollution.

Collecting dew

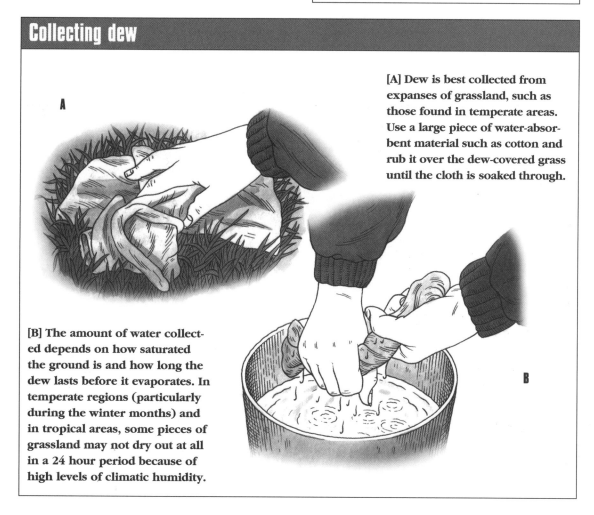

[A] Dew is best collected from expanses of grassland, such as those found in temperate areas. Use a large piece of water-absorbent material such as cotton and rub it over the dew-covered grass until the cloth is soaked through.

[B] The amount of water collected depends on how saturated the ground is and how long the dew lasts before it evaporates. In temperate regions (particularly during the winter months) and in tropical areas, some pieces of grassland may not dry out at all in a 24 hour period because of high levels of climatic humidity.

stiffness in their joints when rain is impending.
- Wooden handles tighten up when rain is about to arrive, and campfire smoke starts swirling more violently.
- 'Red sky at night, shepherds' delight. Red sky in morning, shepherds' warning.' This antique piece of wisdom is actually true. In the morning, a reddened sky tells you that the sun is shining through clouds on the horizon, clouds that will probably bring rain later in the day.

It's a good idea to practise observing all of the above before embarking on a survival adventure or trip. Getting to know nature's moods and habits can give you a real edge in the search for water.

OBTAINING WATER

As stated, there are five main sources of water in any survival environment: open water, water from condensation, falling water, water within plants and underground water.

Open water

Open sources of fresh water – ponds, streams, rivers, snow, ice – are a gift for the survivor as the water is simply there for the

Making a solar still

The two key factors to making a solar still work efficiently are: 1) the seal between the plastic sheet and the soil must have no significant gaps which allow the water moisture to escape the still; 2) the sheet must not touch the walls of the hole otherwise the soil will reabsorb the water droplets as they run down the sheet.

taking. However, before congratulating yourself prematurely, remember that all water sources, regardless of how pure and clear they look, must be purified and filtered before drinking. Almost all will contain aquatic parasites or, even worse, serious waterborne diseases. The worst offenders are pools of still water that stagnate and breed germs and bacteria. A basic rule with all open water sources is that if they are surrounded by dead or dying plants and/or animals, then the water is likely to be polluted or poisonous. Powder or foam deposits washing up at the waterline indicate chemical pollutants, but as a further test it is a good idea to boil off a small quantity of the water to see if any deposits are left when all the water has evaporated. If a river or stream is full of algae and choking amounts of weeds, then agricultural chemicals are the likely suspects. And when cattails and rushes are present in large volumes, it's a clear indication that the water has gone stagnant.

These unpleasant-looking water sources are best left alone, because even filtering and purifying might not remove the hazardous elements. But even if you come across a bright, clear waterhole with plenty of fresh green foliage and lots of animals drinking from it, beware – drinking animals pass parasites into the water. Drinking water containing these parasites can have consequences ranging from unpleasant to fatal, depending on the location.

As long as you bear these precautions in mind, open water is still the best water source. Fill as many containers as possible with the purified water in case of lean times ahead.

One supply of open water, often overlooked, is dew. Dew consists of water droplets that have condensed out of the air overnight. It collects on grass and plants in significant quantities over large areas (many large grazing animals get their water almost exclusively from the dew in grass).

To collect dew, simply run a cloth over the grass, soaking it, and then wring the water out into a container. Repeat the process as often as you need to, but remember to work quickly, as the rising sun will soon cause the dew to evaporate from the land.

Transpiration bag (on a tree)

Transpiration bags can provide up to 0.5 pints (0.25 litres) of fluid per day if well constructed around fresh and growing vegetation. Locate the bags in places which can be easily found later, and make sure that the bag is tied tight around the branch to stop it falling off when the weight of water builds up.

Water from condensation

Wherever we are, water is actually all around us, trapped in tiny particles suspended in the air. However, these particles have no survival value in their airborne state. But getting this vapour to condense in large quantities provides another potentially life-saving and safe source of water. This process of transpiration requires either soil or vegetation. The key piece of kit in both cases is a sheet of plastic (preferably clear), about 3ft (1m) long on each side. Include one in a survival kit as a matter of course.

The first technique to learn is that of constructing a solar still. A solar still works on the principle that if heat is created in an enclosed space, the air will become saturated with vapour and condense in the form of water on the coolest available surface. To build a solar still, first dig a hole about 3ft (1m) in diameter and place a container in the bottom, centred, as a water catcher. Spread your sheet of clear plastic over the hole, securing the perimeter tightly with plenty of heavy rocks and stones. The centre of the sheet should dip down into the hole so that the lowest point hangs directly over the container. Weight the sheet with a stone in the centre to make sure. This is the solar still.

Preparing a transpiration bag (on ground)

This ground-based transpiration system works by trapping water droplets in the gully dug around the vegetation. The water can be drained off at one end into a container, though a better option is to insert a drinking straw into the bag to draw off the water without dismantling the whole device.

During the day, sunlight heats up the soil, releasing water vapour into the hole. The water condenses on the cooler underside of the plastic, forming water droplets that run down into the container. The still also works at night when the sheet is cooled but the trapped air in the hole remains warm. To save having to dismantle the still with every drink, have a tube running from the container under the lip of the plastic. You can simply suck on it when you need a drink. However, be sure to seal the plastic closely around the tube; otherwise any water vapour that builds up will evaporate into the atmosphere.

The principle of the solar still can also be applied to vegetation by tying a plastic bag over a green patch of foliage or a plant. The condensation given off by the plant during photosynthesis (the plant has to be alive and growing for this to work) condenses against the inside of the bag and then runs down to the lowest point, usually the corner of the bag. (Some plastic bags have moulding holes in their base – check for these as they render the bag useless for these survival techniques.) Try to stop the vegetation from actually pressing against the sides of the bag, as it will soak up some of the condensation droplets as they form.

Building a reservoir

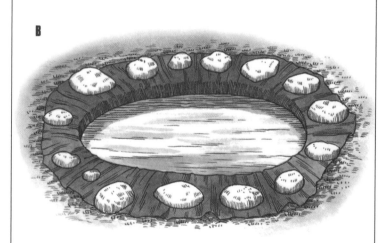

A

B

A personal water reservoir is created by digging a large circular hole in the earth (A), and then lining it with a waterproof sheet (B). (The waterproof sheet will prevent the water from dispersing into the earth.) An improvised lid will help keep animals out, slow water loss to evaporation, and also prevent the green bloom of algae which occurs in any water exposed to sunlight for several days. Do not drink water from the reservoir which is over three or four days old, as it will usually have stagnated.

The importance of salt

As well as water, the human body also requires adequate levels of salt to function properly. A healthy, daily salt intake of about 10gm per day will compensate for natural salt depletion through sweat and urination. Low salt levels cause fatigue, confusion, sickness and muscle cramps. Salt water is the best means of replenishing lost reserves, but do not drink it straight. Instead, either dilute it heavily with fresh water or, preferably, boil it dry to leave a residue of salt crystals. Then add a pinch of this salt to a cup of water. A rather more unpalatable way of getting salt is by adding the blood of creatures you have killed to other foods. Some plants also provide salt, among them the roots of hickory trees in North America or of the Nipa palm in the Far East. Boil the roots and evaporate the water, leaving salt crystals behind.

Another method involves placing the plastic sheet like a tent over a small bush. The edge of the sheet should curl to form a channel circling the bush. This acts as a reservoir for the droplets of condensation. Alternatively, place some foliage inside the plastic bag on a base of stones, making sure to keep the plastic off the vegetation using a stick with a stone on top to raise the 'roof' of the bag clear of the leaves and wood. The stone is not water permeable, so any condensation will collect in the bag and not be reabsorbed by the vegetation.

Extracting water from condensation takes some practice, and should be perfected before you actually need the techniques in a real survival situation. A well-made still may produce about 1US pint/0.8UK pints (0.5 litres) of water a day – not enough to live on (unless you have multiple stills), but certainly enough to keep you going until more secure supplies are found.

Falling water

Rain has the very useful property of being pure and ready to drink as it falls to earth (unless you are in an area of very heavy airborne pollution). Catching it is simply a matter of having as many receptacles open to the downpour as possible, and making them as large as you can. Fashioning gutters out of pieces of bark or waterproof fabric is a useful way of channelling large amounts of water to a single location. The best rain collector is probably a deep hollow carved into the ground and lined with waterproof material, such as a camping groundsheet. Wet clay smeared over the surface of the hole and allowed to dry in advance of any rainfall will also work. When using a groundsheet, make sure that it is firmly in place, weighted with stones or held in place with pegs, as wind often accompanies rainfall.

Underground water

It takes work to get at underground water, so be certain you've chosen the right location before you start digging. Some of these locations have already been outlined earlier: they are basically places where there has previously been water that has now dried up on the surface. Patches of fresh green vegetation indicate underground water. In terms of geological features, explore the following:

● Dry river beds – a dry river bed will often retain underground water beneath the outside edge of a bend, as this is usually the last place from which surface water evaporated. Dig down to underground water.

- Sea shoreline – dig down above the high-tide mark on the beach. The sand will act as a water filter, with fresh water rising above the heavier brine to fill the hole.
- Between sand dunes and in valleys – nature's troughs make natural conduits and receptacles for flowing water, and can prove fruitful sources of underground water.

When digging for water, dig straight down until the earth becomes wet and water starts to seep into the hole. Collect it as it seeps in. Though the water will at first be full of silt, it will eventually become clearer until it is fit for filtering and purification.

Water from plants

We have already seen how transpiration from plants can provide water, but some species of plants actually act as reservoirs themselves for water supplies. Check for sources of water in cup-shaped flowers or leaves, within holes in trees, or even by licking leaves covered in rainwater. (N.B. Be careful that the particular species of plant is not poisonous.)

FILTERING AND PURIFYING WATER

Once water is found and gathered, one vital process remains: filtering and purifying it to make it fit for human consumption. Normal domestic tap water in the UK and the US undergoes rigorous purification processes. Drinking tap water in another country where

Digging for water

Water is found underground in most places, though the depth at which it occurs varies tremendously. In wet tropical or temperate regions it can literally be a few centimetres below the surface, whereas arid desert regions may have watertables tens of metres underground. When digging for water allow the hole to fill up naturally and slowly and always filter and purify the water in case there are contaminants in the soil.

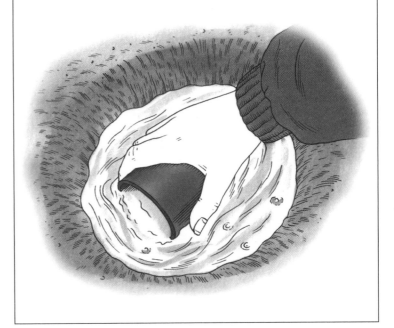

standards are somewhat slacker can result in a severe stomach upset. The consequences of drinking wild water can be even more serious, especially as the diarrhoea brought on by impure water will accelerate dehydration.

The first stage is to filter the water. Pour the water several times through a close-woven piece of fabric – such as cotton – into a container. With this simple process, larger particles of dirt and vegetation, and even some parasites, are caught in the fabric of the cloth. Once the water has been filtered, it has to be purified. The well-prepared survivor will be equipped with an artificial means of purification. This can be in chemical form, which can be added to the water, or a water-purifying device if you have one. The three main chemicals used in water purification are iodine, potassium permanganate and chlorine. We will now look at each of these in turn:

Filtering through a sock

A sock filter is good for straining out larger particles of dirt and vegetation from a sample of water. However, the open knit of many socks will limit its filtering applications, and a tighter material such as cotton is preferred. Using a sock as a filter quickly makes it useless for most other purposes, so it must not be used if socks to wear are in short supply.

Iodine

Iodine usually comes in liquid form in a bottle with a dropper. When iodine is added to water according to the instructions, the water turns slightly pink and acquires a chemical taste, but it is safe to drink.

Potassium Permanganate

This sterilizing chemical is granular in form. As with iodine, enough is added to the water to turn it slightly pink, at which point the water is drinkable.

Chlorine

Many people will be familiar with chlorine in the shape of purifying tablets. Usually, one tablet is added to 1US pint/0.8UKpints (0.5 litres) of water to make it safe to drink, but follow the manufacturer's instructions.

There are a number of very useful treatment machines. The most widely used are purification pumps. One end of the pump is inserted into the source of water, and an outlet tube is placed in a water receptacle. A manually operated plunger draws in dirty water and passes it through purifying chemicals (usually iodine) to pump clear drinking water through the tube into the receptacle.

The cup purifier works on the same principle as the pump, except that a quantity of water is poured into the top of this device. This then filters down into a cup at the bottom of the machine that can be detached for drinking purposes.

The virtue of these devices is that they produce immediate results and require no skill to use. However, in unplanned survival situations, you will have to fall back on the standard method of purification – boiling. After filtering, boil all impure water for a minimum of 10 minutes to kill bacteria.

As soon as you have clean drinking water, drink only what you need and store the rest. Storing water is a skill in itself. There are many excellent varieties of artificial contain-

Using a distillation filter

Distillation filtering is a good way of purifying very polluted or salty water. Water is placed in a boiling vessel which is covered over with thick cloths. Once the water is boiling, the steam soaks into the cloths which are then wrung out into a water container. Pollutants are not carried in the steam so the water which results from the distillation filter is perfectly drinkable.

Containers for storing water

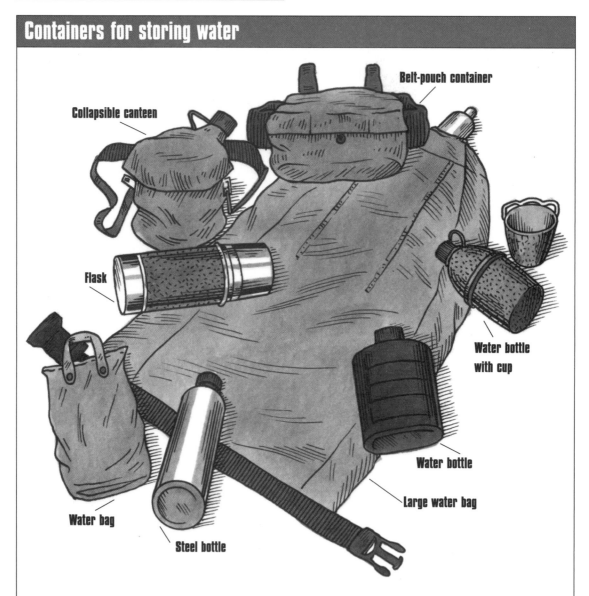

Belt-pouch container

Collapsible canteen

Flask

Water bottle with cup

Water bag

Steel bottle

Water bottle

Large water bag

There are many water containers available, each with its own virtues. Collapsible containers are especially useful because they only take up the space of the water held, though they are not as durable as a rigid-case container. Always take two or three varieties of water container, and include a large water bag amongst your team for long stopovers or survival situations.

ers. For personal use, the best combination is a good plastic water bottle (4US pints/3.5UK pints/2 litres) fitted with a drinking cup. This comes with a large, collapsible water bag for more extensive storage when necessary. These bags can hold up to 30-40US pints/26–35UK pints (15–20 litres), but they fold down small enough to fit into a pack.

If greater storage capacity is needed, there are several ways to improvise. As already described in this chapter, a large pit lined with a waterproof sheet or clay can be used to catch rainwater. This same pit can be used to store water. Remember when digging to go right down to the clay or bedrock lying beneath the soil, as this will stop the water draining away. Another method is to make wooden cups out of the hollowed-out bough sections of trees. These can be waterproofed on the inside by painting them with resin extracted from the bark of birch trees (make cuts in the bark and collect the seeping sap). Birch trees themselves are useful for water storage because their bark is ideal for making large rectangular containers (see box feature).

Whatever storage method you use, keep the water covered over at all times, and in the dark if possible. Even tap water will start to develop green algae if left out in direct sunlight. Remember that if storing pure rainwater, it will need filtering and purifying after a couple of days to remove foreign bodies, parasites and germs.

Water is vital in a survival situation, so make sure you ration it in a sensible and disciplined way. However, if you only have a tiny amount, then drink it all. Rationing a small amount into minuscule daily rations will do nothing to sustain health. A small amount is better off inside you than in a container. The crucial thing is finding more, if at all possible.

One final point concerning water is that respectable amounts are acquired from solid food intake. The amount of water contained in solid foods varies considerably. Water melons, for example, are 93 per cent water, cucumbers are 96 per cent water, and most vegetables are over 90 per cent water.

Even apparently drier fruit and vegetables are water rich – a banana, for example, contains 76 per cent water and a potato 80 per cent. Meat (red meat, poultry and seafood) are between 60 and 80 per cent water, though the amount of water such foods require to digest more than offset the amount they provide.

If very little water is available, then it is best not to eat at all. As water rations grow, however, the diet should be designed, if possible, around water-rich foods until water rations are plentiful.

CHAPTER THREE

Survival food - plant sources

Plants are the most easily accessible survival food, and mostly require little effort to gather and eat. However, confident plant identification is essential to avoid the world's many species of poisonous or inedible plant life.

The earth is host to some 300,000 species of vegetation, with many more sub-species, and about 100,000 species of fungi. Plant life takes many forms: from tiny patches of moss only a few millimetres high, to the greatest of all trees, the giant sequoia known as 'General Sherman' in California, 260ft (80m) high and weighing over 2000 tonnes (2000 tons).

The enormous success of plants in enduring and proliferating upon the earth is due to many factors, including efficient seed dispersal, durability under severe weather conditions and resistance to damage by predators. Plants also have the capacity to produce their own food, usually from the water and carbon dioxide contained in the air, though they further depend on minerals and nutrients extracted from the soil via their roots.

The success story of plant life means that the survivor is rarely in a location where he is that far away from a life-sustaining food source. Edible plants provide almost all essential carbohydrates, proteins, fats (mainly from nuts) and vitamins and minerals (though in most survival situations, limited food choices require meat consumption also). Individual plants may contain many nutrients in their various parts – the seeds, fruit, nuts, roots, stems and leaves.

PLANT IDENTIFICATION

However, not all plants are beneficial. Some plants containing toxins – regardless of their pleasing or benign appearance – can induce severe illness after only a few minutes. The chemicals contained in others, if ingested, will kill within a day. It is therefore important to be able to identify those that are dangerous, even lethal. Unfortunately, identification isn't always that easy.

The first, and most important, stage, in any attempt to become familiar with and knowledgeable about survival plant foods is research. Do not be too ambitious. Choose to learn everything possible about a select few of the most common and easily distinguished edible plants that grow in a type of environment that you intend to visit. The important characteristics include: appearance, distinguishing scents, seasonal changes (these can affect whether the plant is edible or not), locations of growth, (including any other species that often accompany them in those locations), its proper name (so that you can cross-check your information accurately with other reference sources) and the maximum size to which it can grow.

Select a specific area to explore, and a definable natural habitat, such as a wood. Do some more investigation into the plants indigenous to this location and your country. Ask local experts for more information. When you come across a plant that you think might be edible, make sure that it matches all identification criteria – unfortunately, some poisonous plants are similar in appearance to edible vegetation. Only when identification is definite should you proceed to eat the plant according to the proper guidelines.

Avoid any plant that appears sick or diseased – look for discoloration or rot. It is also crucial to bear in mind that not all edible plants are safe to eat because poisons present in the local soil, air or water are often ingested by the plant. So when selecting plants to eat, there are several factors to take into account:

- Avoid plants in areas that have received crop spraying. Also, beware of eating plants from hedgerows bordering crop fields, as these can sometimes collect pesticide sprays through the run-off of water from the field.
- Be careful about eating plants by the sides of busy roads – leave at least 50ft (15m) either side of the road. This is because plants, particularly the stems, leaves and roots, can easily absorb airborne lead. The fruit, berries and nuts are most resistant to lead absorption.
- Do not eat plants growing in or around

Tree bark

The tree bark of several species can provide a fine source of sustenance. Discard the outer bark because it contains high concentrations of tannin, and instead mine the tree for its inner bark. Identify one of the tree species listed below and peel off a section of outer bark near the bottom to reveal sap-rich inner bark (more nutritious sap will be present in the summer than the winter). This bark can be eaten raw or, for easier digestion, boiled. This is a sweet-tasting and delicious meal. When cut into, some trees ooze resin or gum. These sugary substances can be eaten to provide a strong burst of energy. A more refined substance obtained is the syrup obtained from the bark of birch and maple trees. To get useable amounts of sap-like substances, you may have to tap a tree for several days.

Trees with edible inner bark: Aspens (*Populus tremula*); birches (*Betula*); hemlocks (*Tsuga*); maples (*Acer*); pines (*Pinus*); poplars (*Populus*); slippery elm (*Ulmus rubra*); willows (*Salix*).

Digging up roots

Roots are often the most nutritious elements of an edible plant. To dig up a root, first sharpen a long, straight stick from one side so that it forms a chisel-like edge (A). Insert the stick down the side of a plant and chisel away until the root is well exposed (B). Then the stick can be used to lever the root to the surface.

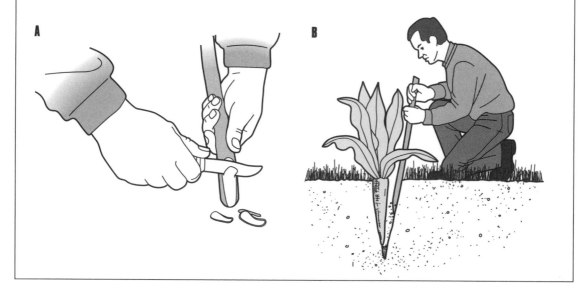

A

B

polluted water. This can be difficult to spot as some agricultural chemicals promote vigorous, healthy-looking plant growth. So, to determine the edibility of the plant, examine the quality of the water.

● Watch out for edible plants brushing up against dangerous, non-edible plants. Keep all individual specimens of plants you collect in separate bags away from other specimens.

● Wash all plants before eating, taking care to remove any solid matter or insect residue.

While collecting and sampling plants in non-survival situations, try to be conservation conscious. Do not collect rare or protected plants (even if they are very common to your area), and take only those parts of the plant that you intend to eat, never the whole plant. As a general rule of thumb, never take more than 10 per cent of the total plant structure. Any more and the plant is likely to die.

LOCATING PLANT FOOD

Locating safe, edible plant food requires an effective strategy. The best approach is to divide the landscape into its different types of terrain, as each offers its own clues as to types of plant that grow there, and where they can be found. There are three basic groups of ecosystem in temperate-climate locations: lawns and meadows; thickets and copses; and woodlands and forests.

Lawns and meadows

With the exception of the United Kingdom and a small number of other countries, there are few natural lawns in the world. Most are cultivated around human habitats, which usually results in the destruction of many of the plant species often found in untended grassland. Nevertheless, despite intense cutting, lawns can still yield some varieties of survival food, including dandelions, plantains and pepper grasses. And when a piece of grassland, for example a meadow, is left untended, the number of edible plant foods – particularly herbaceous biennials – increases dramatically. Primroses, buckwheat, wild carrot, stinging nettle, curled dock and a whole host of shrubs and large plants – including isolated trees – will flourish, making a meadow rich with natural sources of nutrition.

Thickets and copses
Dense clumps of vegetation tend to feature small, woody plants. Usefully, this category of plant is a source of much low-lying fruit production, such as blackberries, raspberries, wild roses, groundnut, nettles and common plantain. The added benefit is that thickets and copses concentrate all their resources in one small patch.

Woodland and forests
Woodlands and forest are obviously the richest sources of survival plant food merely because of the concentration of plant species within the ecosystem. One of the greatest advantages of attempting to survive in a densely wooded area is that it will provide you with food in all seasons. While in spring, you might be tucking into the young leaves of violet or hawthorn, rosehips and cat's-tail are on the menu in darkest winter.

Making drinks from plants

Certain plant substances, such as pine needles, are suitable for producing drinks through the infusion method. Using two teaspoons of pine needles per cup, crush the needles with a large stone to release their flavours (A). Then tip the needles into boiling water and allow the mix to sit for up to 10 minutes, stirring occasionally (B). Finally, strain the fluid through a piece of cloth into a vessel and drink (C).

A

B

C

EATING PLANTS

There are times when it is impossible to memorize by heart the key identification features of all the world's plants. And of course you might find yourself in an environment with none of the plants you know or subspecies with subtle but unfamiliar variations. This is especially the case in jungles.

In such situations, therefore, it is important to know some general guidelines about what is safe to eat and what is not. These rules are not failsafe and should be backed up by sound knowledge of various plant species and the Universal Edibility Test (see feature on page 52). That said, they are the rules taught to military special forces and aviators as part of their survival training, and have proved their worth in many real survival situations.

- Avoid eating bulbs unless you know positively that they are safe.
- When deciding whether berries are edible, use the following rules: white and yellow berries are usually poisonous; 50 per cent of red berries are poisonous; and blue and black berries are usually safe to eat.
- Single pieces of fruit hanging from a stem are usually safe to eat.
- Don't eat a plant that issues a milky white sap unless you can identify it as an edible species (such as dandelion).
- Fruit divided into five segments is usually unsafe.
- Avoid plants with tiny barbed hairs stuck to the stem and leaves, as these will act as irritants on the throat and may be tipped with stinging chemicals.
- Generally avoid red plants.
- Don't eat plants that irritate your skin.

Follow the above guidelines and ignore other 'word-of-mouth advice' that you may have heard, especially the 'tip' that it is possible to judge which plants are safe to eat by observing what the local animals eat. This is actually a very good way of ending up either ill or dead. The digestive systems of many animals can process foodstuffs that are hazardous to humans. Even our closest relatives, the primates, can tolerate bacteria and germs that would make us seriously ill.

POISON

In the plant kingdom, there are two particular poisons that pose a perennial danger: hydrocyanic acid and oxalic acid. Hydrocyanic acid, also known as prussic acid, is highly toxic and dangerous to human health. Plants containing this acid have a distinctive smell of bitter almonds or peaches – crush some of the leaves to see if they give off this smell. Plants containing hydrocyanic acid include cherry laurel and plants that are normally edible – such as raspberry, cherry, peach, blackberry and plum – when they are old and wilted. Avoid any of these plants when they are in a decayed state, and test the scent of all plants you are tempted to eat if you aren't entirely sure of the species.

Oxalic acid has no scent but instead causes a burning or stinging sensation on contact with skin. So, test all plant materials you intend to eat by rubbing them on a patch of skin and waiting for a few moments for a reaction (stinging, burning or blistering). Plants containing oxalic acid include wild rhubarb and wild sorrel.

COOKING

Having finally gathered a safe and edible plant, it's time to decide whether it should be cooked or not. Some parts of plants need no cooking, such as the fruit or nut, which contain edible matter inside a protective skin or shell. However, cooking other plant food is usually essential not only to make it palatable, but also to destroy germs and disease-bearing bacteria.

With greens, boiling is usually the preferred method of cooking. Boiling removes much of the bitterness in the leaves, makes them easy to digest and kills most harmful bacteria after 10 minutes. With plants that are extra bitter, it may be necessary to change the water several times in the cooking process to achieve a more pleasant taste. Even this may not be wholly successful. If not, mix the plant with other ingredients in a soup or stew to subdue its flavour. Greens that are not bitter should be steamed or boiled in shallow water for as long as it takes for them to be cooked. Boiling for too long will kill off almost all the plant's essential vitamins. The water that you boil plants in is often nutritious, so drink it rather than throw it away.

Roots are amongst the plant world's most versatile foodstuff when it comes to cooking. Treat them exactly as you would potatoes – boil, mash or fry them, or try a combination. A particularly good combination is to parboil the root, then roast it on hot stones until soft. Whichever method you choose, make sure that all roots are cooked thoroughly because some contain harmful substances when raw. Try not to peel roots – the most nutritious elements are often contained in the skin.

Selected edible plants

Plant name: Bistorts (*Polygonum*)
Description: Grows to a height of 12–24in (30–60cm). Narrow leaves with triangular shape. Slim cluster of pink or white flowers.
Location: Grassy areas and woodland.
Eating notes: Soak roots, then roast.

Plant name: Blackberries and wild raspberries (*Rubus*)
Description: Familiar straggly bushes with snagging thorns. Blackberry fruit ripens from green through red to black during the summer months; raspberry ripens early to red.
Location: Woodlands, waste ground and copses.
Eating notes: Eat fruit raw after washing.

Plant name: Bracken (*Pteridum aquilinum*)
Description: Large leafy fronds growing in dense clumps and sections.

Universal edibility test

The following test can be used to establish the safety of plant food if its identity is uncertain. You should only use this test in extreme situations and never apply it to fungi.

- Select only one part of a plant to test and do not eat anything else for the duration of the test. Drink only water.
- Hold the plant against the inside of your forearm for about 15 minutes to see if there is an adverse skin reaction. If not, proceed with the test.
- Take a small piece of the plant and touch it against your lips. Wait five minutes to see if there is an allergic reaction.
- Place the piece of plant on your tongue. Hold it there for three minutes. If there is no reaction, chew the plant but do not swallow. Hold it in your mouth for a full 15 minutes.
- If there is no reaction, swallow. Wait for about eight hours to see if a reaction develops. If not, eat a small handful of the plant prepared in exactly the same way.
- Wait another eight hours. If no reaction develops – mild or adverse – then the plant should be safe to eat.

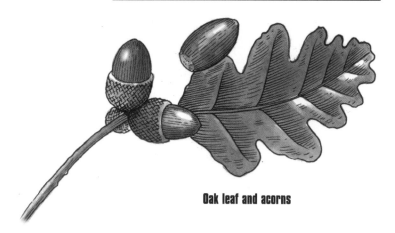

Oak leaf and acorns

Location: Almost universal – one of the world's most successful plant forms.

Eating notes: Only young 'fiddlehead' shoots are edible – older bracken is poisonous. Boil the young shoots for a half hour after removing the woody parts. Do not eat large amounts. Roots can be boiled or roasted.

Plant name: Buckwheat (*Fagopyrum esculentum*)
Description: Grows to about 24in (60cm). Stems usually red. Small flowers, pink or white. Spear-shaped leaves.
Location: Grassy areas.
Eating notes: Use the seed for an edible grain.

Plant name: Cat's-tail (*Typha*)
Description: Grows to 6–15ft (2–5m). Distinguished by tubular, sausage-like flower head and long, narrow leaves.
Location: In and around fresh water sources.
Eating notes: Rootstock and stem, raw or boiled. Boil leaves and young shoots.

Plant name: Chickweed (*Stellaria media*)
Description: Grows to 12in (30cm). Pointed oval leaves and very small, five-petalled, white flowers. Stem features a line of hairs.
Location: Grassy and waste areas.
Eating notes: Boil the leaves.

Plant name: Dandelion (*Taraxacum*)
Description: Large yellow to orange flowers with dense petal pattern on long stalks. Deeply lobed leaves; jagged.
Location: Universal.
Eating notes: Young leaves can be eaten raw; older leaves require boiling (change

water to remove bitterness). Roots can be boiled. Excellent survival food.

Plant name: Good King Henry (*Chenopodium bonus-henricus*)
Description: Grows up to 24in (60cm) tall. Green triangular leaves that can redden. Spikes of tiny green flowers.
Location: Grassy and waste areas.
Eating notes: Eat leaves and young shoots, boiled or raw. Young shoots should be peeled.

Plant name: Groundnut (*Apios americana*)
Description: A vine-like plant with oval, pointed leaves. Flowers – varying shades of reddish brown.
Location: Mainly North America. Moist woodland.
Eating notes: Peel and cook, then roast or boil the small tubers.

Plant name: Hawthorn (*Crataegus*)
Description: Small tree or shrub. Red fruit in the fall (autumn) accompanied by deep-lobed green leaves. White or pink flowers.
Location: Waste ground and wooded areas.
Eating notes: Raw fruit is edible.

Plant name: Jerusalem artichoke (*Helianthus tuberosus*)
Description: A very tall plant that flowers

Stinging nettles

with a large, circular, yellow flower. Large oval leaves. Similar in appearance to a sunflower.
Location: Mainly wasteground in North America.
Eating notes: Cook, but do not peel, the tubers.

Plant name: Juniper (*Juniperus communis*)
Description: Woody shrub about 15ft (5m) tall or low-lying bush with needle-type leaves and small berries ripening from green through to blue-black.
Location: Found in mountainous and northern regions.
Eating notes: Eat only the ripe fruit; cook to make more palatable.

Plant name: Oak (*Quercus*)
Description: Familiar tree that can grow to enormous size with deeply lobed leaves and acorns.
Location: Throughout the temperate world.
Eating notes: Shell acorns and boil in several changes of water (or soak in cold water for several days). Roast to eat – cooked and ground acorns can also substitute for flour and coffee.

Plant name: Pine (*Pinus*)
Description: Tall, easily recognisable 'Christmas' tree with needle leaves and pine cones.
Location: Throughout most temperate locations.
Eating notes: Collect mature pine cones and heat. This releases seeds that can be eaten raw or roasted. Needles can also be boiled to make a nutritious drink.

Plant name: Primose (*Primula*)
Description: Crinkly basal leaves that taper to a rounded end. Five-petalled flowers on long stalks, mostly shades of yellow but also pink.
Location: Fields, woods and hedgerows throughout most of the temperate world.
Eating notes: Whole plant is edible but the leaves are the best. Boil.

Plant name: Reeds (*Phragmites*)
Description: Slim, long, grey-green leaves. Brown-purple, feathery flower heads. Grows to 13ft (4m).
Location: In and around fresh water.
Eating notes: Roots are edible; boil.

Plant name: Stinging nettles (*Urtica*)
Description: Oval leaves, toothed around the edges and covered with fine, stinging hairs. Green flowers.
Location: Almost universal.
Eating notes: Eat plants when young (6–8in /15–20cm high), or young offshoots. Boil for

at least six minutes; this destroys the stinging acid in the leaves. If dried, leaves can be used as a stored food.

Plant name: Sweet chestnuts (*Castenea*)
Description: Tree grows up to 90ft (30m). Large, pointed, toothed leaves. Tree produces catkins and nuts in a thick, green, spiky husk. (Do not confuse this plant with the horse chestnut, which has poisonous nuts. Refer to an identification guide.)
Location: Woodland.
Eating notes: Break open husks, remove nuts and peel, boil and mash.

Plant name: Walnut (*Juglans*)
Description: Tree grows up to 90ft (30m) with furrowed bark and toothed, narrow leaflets. Brown nuts, at first contained in a green husk.
Location: Most temperate regions.
Eating notes: Nuts give excellent nutrition and energy. Eat raw or roasted.

Plant name: Water chestnut (*Trapa natans*)
Description: An aquatic plant. Diamond-shaped leaves float on the water. Small, white flowers.
Location: Fresh water locations throughout Europe and Asia.
Eating notes: Features hard, grey seeds with two-horned shape; these can be eaten uncooked or roasted.

Plant name: White mustard (*Synapsis alba*)
Description: Plant grows up to 24in (60cm). Hairy stem and crinkly leaves with deep lobes. Pale-yellow flowers.
Location: Grassland and waste areas throughout Europe and Asia.
Eating notes: The leaves and flowers can be eaten raw when young. Cooking makes the whole plant edible.

Plant name: Wild onions (*Allium*)
Description: Long stem like dandelion with long, very narrow leaves extending from the base. Six-petalled, pink, purple or white flowers. Gives off the distinctive onion smell.
Location: Found in most places in temperate regions.
Eating notes: Edible onion bulb located underground at a depth of about 10in (25cm).

Plant name: Wild parsnips (*Pastinaca sativa*)
Description: Grows to a height of about 3ft (1m). Toothed broad leaflets, pungent smell. Dense clusters of small, yellow flowers at the end of a stalk.
Location: Grassy areas and wasteland.
Eating notes: Roots are edible raw or cooked.

Plant name: Wild roses (*Rosa*)
Description: Resemble poor-quality garden roses with white or pink flowers and thorny stems.

Raspberries and blackberries

Poisonous plants to avoid (temperate zones)

Three poisonous plants common to temperate areas. If ingested, Foxglove interferes with the heart and causes arrhythmia and possible seizures, while Water

Hemlock and Deadly Nightshade can be fatal even if only one mouthful is eaten. All parts of these plants are toxic. Memorize their appearance and stay clear of them.

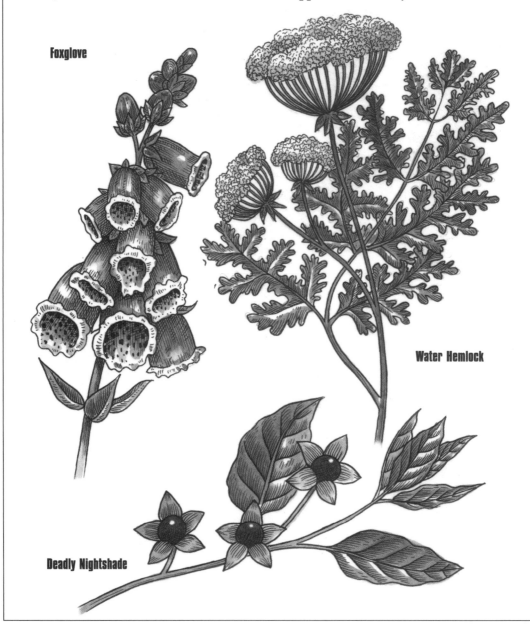

Foxglove

Water Hemlock

Deadly Nightshade

Location: Throughout temperate world.
Eating notes: Red seedcases (hips) can be eaten raw, or boiled to make a syrup. Very high in vitamin C.

Plant name: Wild Sorrel (*Rumex acetosa*)
Description: Grows to about 3ft (1m). Long, arrow-shaped leaves. Very small, red and green flowers set on spikes.
Location: Grassy areas and wasteland.
Eating notes: Eat while young. Leaves can be eaten raw but boiling makes them more palatable.

The list of plants given here just scratches the surface of the edible larder out there in the wild. However much time you spend familiarizing yourself with these plants, make sure that you invest an equal amount of time in learning about the varieties of poisonous plants. Those found in temperate climates that you should become particularly familiar with are: baneberries (*Actaea*), deadly nightshade (*Atropa belladonna*), death camus (*Zigadenus venosus*), foxglove (*Digitalis*), hemlock (*Conium maculatum*), monk's hood (*Aconitum*), thorn-apple (*Datura stramonium*) and water hemlocks or cowbanes (*Cicuta*).

FUNGI AS SURVIVAL FOOD

Edible forms of fungi are excellent survival foods. They are usually high in vitamins and minerals – typically vitamins A, the B complex, C and D, and the mineral phosphorus. They also contain more protein than other vegetables (though not quite as much as meat), can provide decent amounts of fat and are easily gathered, all of which makes them worth seeking out. However, many species of fungi are poisonous, and some are outright lethal.

With poisonous fungi, cooking does not destroy their poisons. N.B. the Universal Edibility Test does not work with fungi. A fungus like death cap, if ingested, results in

Field mushroom

death from liver failure in 90 per cent of cases after a hideous week of excruciating illness. With so much more at stake, the rules for eating fungi are strict.

The primary rule is that you do not eat any fungi that you cannot positively identify. There are some general rules: don't eat fungi that have white gills, a volva (a cup-like structure attached to the base of the stem) or rings around the stem. Also, don't eat an otherwise edible fungus when it is old or decomposing. Fungi fall rigidly into either edible or inedible varieties. Consult the illustrations in this chapter and other relevant sources to determine which fungi belong to which category. Only use high-quality illustrations and detailed descriptions to build up your knowledge. Also pay a visit to a good botanical garden; they often have fungi sections that allow you to see the plants close up.

There are two basic categories of fungi: ground fungi (which grow out of the earth) and bracket fungi (which grow out of the side of a tree). Both categories contain edible and poisonous varieties.

If in the wild you have identified an edible fungus, you should clean it thoroughly, removing any discoloured or decaying parts. Softer varieties of fungi – usually ground fungi – can be used in soups and stews, or even eaten raw. Tougher bracket fungi may require some soaking in cold water first to soften them up. Fungi can also be dried for later use by placing the separated caps and stems on a rock in the sun until they have dehydrated. In this dry state, they will keep for days in an airtight container. To rehydrate for eating, simply soak them in water.

Here are two lists of the edible and inedible fungi that a survivor might find in temperate-climate zones. Neither list is exhaustive.

Edible fungi
Beefsteak fungus (*Fistulina hepatica*);
chanterelle (*Cantharellus cibarius*);
dryad's saddle (*Polyporus squamosus*);
field mushroom (*Agaricus augustus*);
giant puffball (*Lycoperdon giantea*);
honey or bootlace fungus
  (*Armillaria mellea*);
horn of plenty (*Craterellus cornucopioides*);
horse mushroom (*Agaricus arvensis*);

oyster fungus (*Pleurotus ostreatus*);
parasol mushroom (*Lepiota procera*);
wood mushroom (*Agaricus sylvestris*).

Poisonous fungi
Death cap (*Amanita phalloides*);
destroying angel (*Amanite virosa*);
fly agaric (*Amanita muscaria*);
leaden entoloma (*Entoloma sinnuatum*);
panther cap (*Amanita pantherina*);
yellow staining mushroom
  (*Agaricus sylvestris*);
Cortinarius speciosissimus; Inocybe patouillardi; Paxilus involutus

STORING AND PRESERVING PLANT FOOD
In an ideal world, survival foraging will yield more sources of food than can be eaten. In prolonged survival situations, leave any surplus food growing in its natural state, because it will start to decay as soon as it's picked. Remember, however, that you are competing for food with wild animals. If a food source has to be picked because it is likely to get picked clean by the local wildlife, or it needs to be moved to another location, then it must be preserved.

The first rule is that picked plant food should be kept from getting wet, as this usually accelerates the process of decomposition. Keeping the foods in airtight containers and in the dark will also help preservation. Drying out plant foods will increase their storage time enormously. Fruit and fungi are easily dried out. Either leave them exposed to the sun on a rock (keep watch over them in case birds pick them off, and protect them from rain and dew), or suspend the pieces over a smoky fire (though not close enough to cook them). Both these methods provide a dehydrated food source that can be rehydrated simply by soaking it in water

Giant puffball

Poisonous fungi (temperate zones)

Death Cap and Destroying Angel are two of the most deadly fungi found in temperate regions. Death Cap is found in deciduous woodland and is distinguished by a greenish-olive cap set upon a paler stem with a large volva. Destroying Angel is entirely white, has a flaky stem and has a sweet odour. The caps of both types grow to 5in (12cm) across. These fungi are quite lethal if ingested.

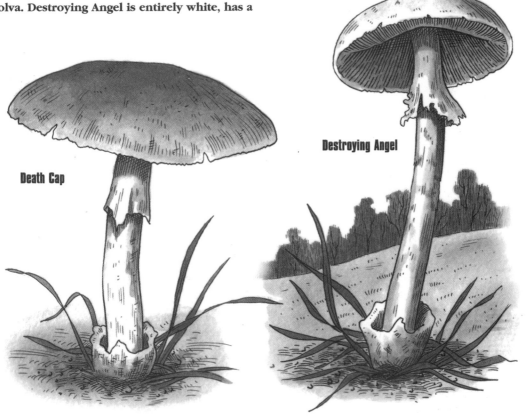

Death Cap

Destroying Angel

until soft. Be aware, however, that drying fruit on a rock may take up to 10 days. In general, air-drying will also be impossible if there are high levels of moisture in the air. Keep flies away during this time, because once they have laid their eggs on food, it is effectively inedible.

It is also possible to preserve fruits. Many fruits contain a chemical called pectin. If these fruits are boiled, the acid released reacts with the pectin to form a jelly when it cools. So, by boiling up fruit and storing it in an air-tight container, you have a nutritious food source that stays edible for several weeks.

CHAPTER FOUR

Survival food – animal sources

Meat provides high concentrations of protein and fats for the survivor. In most natural environments plant foods alone will not keep the survivor alive in the long term, so he or she must be prepared to hunt and kill for food.

Most people in the developed world are unaccustomed to the reality of killing living creatures. Meat is purchased straight from the supermarket, clean, neatly packaged and with no hint of the reality of slaughter. In addition, colossal agricultural output has made vegetarianism a real moral option for many people. But in over 70 per cent of the earth's natural habitats, a survivor must kill and eat animals if he is to survive. Nature is a competitive environment, which makes it very difficult to find enough wild plant foods of the right variety to sustain long-term health (though short-term provision is perfectly feasible). In fact, some environments are almost entirely bereft of plant food. The traditional Eskimo peoples of the Arctic, for example, have a 98 per cent meat-based diet, derived mainly from fish and seals. So as a survivor, you will almost certainly have to kill to eat.

ANIMALS AS FOOD

Meat provides large quantities of protein and fat, both of which are essential for energy and body warmth. No vegetable (even nuts) can equal the quantities to be obtained from meat. Meats also contain most of the major vitamins and minerals, though some types of meat provide more than others. Oily fish and liver are excellent, as are eggs. Meat does not contain vitamin C, which is found in fruit and vegetables. As with vegetables, never rely exclusively on one kind of meat to survive.

Eating meat has its advantages and disadvantages. Perhaps the greatest advantage with animals as a food source is their sheer number. At present, there are around two million species of animals in existence. Animal population densities vary enormously – the tropical rain forests alone may well contain nearly one million of these species, whereas only a handful are to be found on the arctic tundra. But animals inhabit every natural environment on earth and their prolific presence means that a food source is rarely far away. The other main advantage with animal food is that the problem of identifying edible species is nowhere near as difficult as it is with plants. Apart from snakes and some species of lizards, spiders, scorpions and insects, almost all land creatures are edible, particularly mammals.

Before going on a survival expedition, find out as much as you possibly can about the animal species indigenous to your intended destination. Familiarize yourself with every aspect of their behaviour, because this will give you an advantage when hunting and tracking.

Sea life presents a slightly different challenge, as some of the world's most poisonous creatures live there. But even there, staying away from brightly coloured or aggressive-looking fish can usually ensure that you still have a safe meal.

The animal kingdom contains a bewildering variety of creatures. The major subsections of this kingdom are: mammals, birds, reptiles, amphibians, fish and invertebrates (including insects). This rich variety is actually good news for the survivor. An unarmed or unskilled survivor, or one too weak from hunger or injury to catch large mammals, can forage for ground-dwelling insects for survival. If he doesn't have a gun or spear, he can trap birds using a net.

Animals also have uses beyond sustenance. The bones, skin and fur, of mammals in particular, can be turned into survival tools or resources. When butchering any animal, do not throw anything away unless it is a health hazard. Fish bones can be used as needles, while larger mammal bones can be

used to make a range of tools, from clubs to saws. Hold on to the skin and fur, but wash and clean them to get rid of parasites (infested skins should be boiled), and then dry them. They can then be used in the construction of shelters and as clothing.

A major benefit of animal foods is that they seem to raise morale significantly. Many kinds of meat can taste quite fantastic when simply cooked over an open fire. In addition, a large kill such as a sheep or wild pig will feed an entire group, which can have a tremendous impact on the group's wellbeing. Wellbeing is not a fanciful irrelevance in a survival situation; high morale can make all the difference between living and dying. Meat is also one of the best food sources for obtaining vitamin B. Vitamin B plays a vital role in the human body, regulating the function of the nervous system, maintaining muscle function, assisting the immune system and helping the breakdown of fats and proteins during digestion.

Though the advantages of animal food far outweigh the disadvantages, there are some negatives. First, and most obvious, is that you have to kill something to eat it. For those not used to it, killing can be a traumatic experience. The best way to cope with this unfamiliar stress is to be clear about your new status as a survivor. Every day, animals slaughter other animals in their millions, usually with greater savagery than is ever deployed by the human hunter. As a survivor, you must assume your natural place in this life cycle. In this way, killing becomes an act central to the scheme of life, and not some hideous moral aberration. Besides, all ethical considerations regarding other living creatures will soon give way to a much harder attitude once actual hunger begins to bite.

A much more practical problem is that animals generally fight back. Therefore, decide which animals you are going to tackle on the basis of their capacity to defend themselves. Animals – apart, perhaps, from dolphins and primates – have no conscience, and, when angered or scared, they will fight with ferocity that humans can rarely equal. Before closing in on any animal for the kill, ask yourself these questions:

- Has it a reputation for violent resistance?
- What is its main mechanism of attack? Consider everything here: teeth, poison, tail (which can deliver whipping injuries), powerful limbs, horns, irritating hairs and a bony skull used for ramming.
- Is the animal solitary or does it live in a group? Attacking one animal can bring others to its defence.
- Does the creature have young? Mammals, reptiles and birds of prey can be especially vicious in the protection of young offspring or eggs.

- If the attack goes wrong, can I get away? Some creatures will pursue you for great distances. Don't, for example, attempt to escape from a bear you have wounded by climbing a tree – it will be a much better climber than you.

Answering these questions before you act will force you to tackle your prey in the safest, most appropriate way, and, possibly, spare you some serious regret. Go for animals that you know you can handle.

Another danger to be wary of with animal meat is the risk of being poisoned. Most species of animal are safe to eat when properly cooked, but not necessarily every individual creature. In particular, be on the lookout out for diseased animals. Tell-tale signs to watch out for include: difficulty moving or

Carrying a killed animal

A large mammal carcass can be transported between two people on a long pole. The animal's legs should be bound securely with rope just above the main joints and the pole is inserted between the ropes and the torso. More rope is used to lash the animal's full body length to the pole, after which the pole can be picked up and the animal suspended from it.

Cuts of meat from a cow

The diagram illustrates the portions of meat into which a large animal carcass is usually divided. The best steak cuts are the fillet (H), rump (G) and sirloin (F) while the silverside (I) yields good roasting joints. Tougher meats which require slow stewing, roasting or boiling are topside (J), hind flank (P), flank (D), brisket (N), clod (L), chuck and blade (B) and leg (K). Of course, all these parts are perfectly edible in a survival situation.

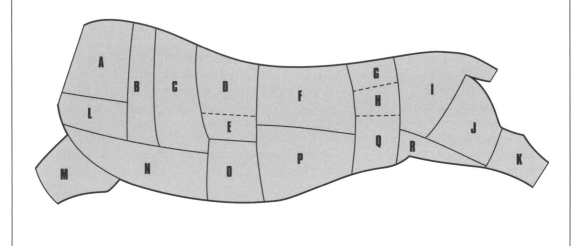

The benefits of eating offal

Offal is often wrongly regarded as the disposable parts of an animal, when actually it is some of the most nutritious. However, a little knowledge is needed to prepare offal properly. The three most valuable kinds of offal are the liver, kidneys and heart. The heart can simply be roasted, or diced and boiled. With liver, you must remove the bile bladder at its centre – it can be pulled off easily using just a finger. Do not eat any liver that is discoloured or that has white spots (signs of disease), and cook it lightly by boiling, roasting or frying. The kidneys require boiling, and you can also use the fat surrounding them to make pemmican. Together, the heart, liver and kidneys have the highest food values of offal, but there are other forms that are usable. Lungs are edible as long as they are pink and healthy looking, though they are not a great source of nutrition. Boil to cook. Intestines can be used as sausage skins by turning them inside out, removing the contents and then boiling. The remaining 'skins' can then be stuffed with a mix of fat and meat prior to boiling once more to cook. To eat stomach, remove the contents, wash and then boil. Incidentally, the partly digested stomach contents can also be boiled to make a meal, a meal that is easily digested as the animal has already done some of the work.

odd behaviour; isolation from the herd or pack; fur or skin in bad condition; and obvious signs such as vomiting or general weakness. In larger mammals such as deer, look to see if the lymph nodes in the cheeks are very swollen. If they are, it is a sign that the animal is fighting some illness or disease (in the same way that the lymph nodes in our throats swell up when we have viruses). Also check the shape of the head, and do not eat the animal if its head is misshapen or discoloured.

Of course, the greatest health risk from meat is that of general food poisoning. Make sure that all meats are thoroughly cooked (there are no rare steaks in survival!). Butcher the animal into useable meats as soon as it is killed. If you cannot preserve the meat by smoking or drying, eat it immediately, especially in hot climates, where decay will begin within hours.

Protect the meat from flies, as these will lay eggs on the meat that will spoil it very quickly. Wrap the meat in either a plastic bag or a piece of cloth, but wash the material out before reusing to clean it of any germs and bacteria. Better still, put the meat in an air-tight container if available.

ANIMAL SPECIES AND FOOD

When in the field, it is best to divide your efforts at collecting meat between a range of the sources at your disposal, which can include: mammals, reptiles, amphibians, birds, invertebrates and fish.

MAMMALS

Mammals can provide meat in greater quantities than most other creatures and are also more accessible than elusive reptiles or birds. There are 4475 certified species of mammal (including humans), which vary enormously in terms of size, behaviour and anatomy. Features common to mammals are a hinged lower jaw, mobile, external ears and body hair. Though the young of most mam-

mals are born fully formed, a small group known as monotremes (represented only by the duck-billed platypus and echidnas) do lay eggs. Mammals are also endothermes, which means that they maintain a constant internal body temperature through a mixture of internal physiological reactions and external behavioural responses. This complex activity requires large amounts of food. Mammals are divided into carnivores, herbivores and omnivores.

Mammals are generally credited with being the most intelligent creatures upon earth. Certainly, many kinds of mammals communicate vocally, and by scent, touch and body language. They have reasonably advanced social structures that involve clear hierarchies, which in turn influence access to mates and food. As a result they are adaptive creatures that can, with varying degrees of success, learn from their environment and respond intelligently to it. Most mammals are quadrupeds (four-footed), though some are bipeds (two-footed). Bats can fly, while whales, dolphins and porpoises can, of course, swim.

The following are the most common forms of mammal to be found in temperate areas:

Badgers

Various species of badger are to be found throughout most of the world. For many people, they are a familiar and welcome sight, but they should be approached with extreme caution. Badgers have very powerful jaws and claws, and can inflict serious, even fatal, injury in a confrontation. Use only passive hunting methods such as deadfalls and snares, and be very sure that the animal is dead before you retrieve it – poke it with a stick or spear from a safe distance.

Cattle

It's the ambitious survivor who will attempt to hunt cattle, but the massive quantity of

Bleeding a deer

Bleeding animal carcasses helps preserve the meat by reducing the animal's fluid content and extracts a useful food in the blood itself. A deer is bled suspended by its rear legs from a wooden frame, its carotid artery in the neck slashed. The frame must be of very solid construction to take the deer's weight; the bough of a tree may be a more convenient alternative.

quality meat they provide may well make it worth the effort. Repeated assaults with spears and bow and arrows may bring the animal to its knees through blood loss over a period of time. However, it will most likely take deadfall traps to take down these enor-mous, impressively strong creatures. Cattle may appear docile, but many will charge you if threatened, and some can achieve speeds of up to 30mph (48km/h) over short dis-tances. Be particularly cautious when near bulls or cattle with calves.

Skinning a rabbit

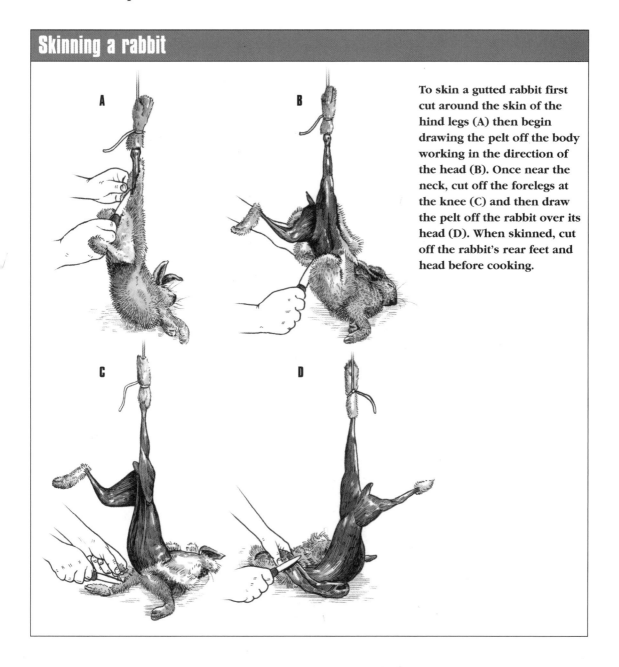

To skin a gutted rabbit first cut around the skin of the hind legs (A) then begin drawing the pelt off the body working in the direction of the head (B). Once near the neck, cut off the forelegs at the knee (C) and then draw the pelt off the rabbit over its head (D). When skinned, cut off the rabbit's rear feet and head before cooking.

Deer

In temperate zones, adult deer range in length from 28–39in (70–100cm) (the alpine musk deer) to 11ft (3.5m) (the mighty elk of North America and Asia). The smaller the deer, the more likely it is to be a solitary creature. Such breeds are to be found mainly in areas where food is sparse and competition extreme. Almost all deer, however, live in wooded areas, and are most active at dawn and dusk. Like wild sheep and goats, their senses, especially hearing and smell, are highly tuned, so you will have to rely on deadfall traps and snares baited with offal, or long-distance projectile weapons. Watch out for deer with antlers; they are purposely designed for combat, and can inflict terrible injuries.

Hedgehogs

Hedgehogs inhabit many regions except the Americas. Once spotted, they are easy to catch, usually just by picking them up straight off the ground. That said, their nocturnal nature makes them elusive. They are agile climbers, so try to stop them escaping into undergrowth or up trees. European hedgehogs tend to curl up into tight balls as a defensive measure, turning their spines outward for protection. Because hedgehogs are usually infested with parasites, always take care when picking them up. A puncture wound from one of the spines may result in serious infection. To make sure you kill all parasites, cook hedgehogs thoroughly. Mud cooking is a good technique for cooking hedgehogs because the baked mud takes the spines with it when it is peeled off.

Rabbits and hares

Rabbits and hares are the all-time survival favourite. Despite the warnings about 'rabbit starvation' noted in chapter one, rabbits still make an excellent survival food. They are to be found in almost every conceivable climate, from the desert to the Arctic, and often in large numbers. A simple snare, set outside a burrow or along a rabbit run, is enough to catch rabbits. Infant rabbits can even be picked up straight from the ground when they go catatonic through the fear brought on by your presence. Hares, being faster and stronger, are more of a challenge, but a simple snare will be effective here too. Use a bola missile or a throwing stick against rabbits and hares on the run.

Sheep and goats

There is a world of difference between wild sheep and goats, and those herded in flocks by farmers. Tended sheep tend to be docile and are easily killed for their meat and wool. This book does not advocate the wanton killing of farmers' livestock but in extreme survival situations it may be necessary. Run down the animal, straddle its back, pull its head up to expose the throat, and cut deeply either side of the windpipe to sever the carotid arteries. Wild sheep and goats pose a far greater challenge. They tend to live in places inaccessible or dangerous to humans, often in mountainous areas with adverse geological and weather conditions. They are also extremely surefooted and quick, while the combined instincts and senses of the herd act as an effective guard against stalkers. Use snares or medium- to long-range projectile weapons to kill, but don't make endless attempts if you are repeatedly outwitted.

Squirrels

Unless you have a firearm or another, equally accurate projectile weapon, it is difficult to catch squirrels because they dart and leap across the uppermost branches of trees. However, if caught in the open on flat ground, they are not so fast and can be killed with a well-aimed stone, stick or bola missile. But the best method of catching these fast-moving tree-dwellers is a spring snare baited with fruit or a bird's egg. Set the snare on a branch that the squirrels frequently use to get from one tree to another.

The art of smoking food

A smoke house is ideal for drying out pieces of meat and vegetables. The most important ingredient for effective smoking is the fuel – it must smoulder, not burn, and produce plentiful smoke. Green hardwood leaves are the best; they are added to the fire once it has burnt low. The frame can be covered over with a leafy bough to concentrate the smoke.

This list of mammals includes many of the most common creatures that survivors can depend on for food. There are, of course, a great many others, and before you embark on a survival adventure, you should spend time studying the wildlife of the region you intend to visit.

Wild dogs

Feral dogs, wolves and foxes are cunning and

Hiding a kill in a tree

An animal which is caught and killed should be butchered immediately if possible. If this is not an option (perhaps there are predators in the area), then it can be placed in a tree to hide or protect it temporarily from ground-dwelling predators. Do not throw the animal up into the tree, as you need to climb up to retrieve it afterwards.

nimble creatures with a powerful sense of smell, hearing and sight, all of which can alert them to a human presence from great distances. Catching any of these creatures means relying instead on snares and nooses baited with meat (canines are very curious). Their meat is fairly tough and will need some boiling. When preparing rump meat, remove the anal glands by cutting around them – do not nick them with the knife as this will release their foul contents.

Wild pigs

Wild pigs inhabit woods and forests, generally in small groups. They provide an excellent meal, especially in the winter, when their fat reserves are high. The best time to hunt them is usually when they are asleep, usually when the day is at its hottest – often you will actually hear snores coming from under thick undergrowth. But wild pigs are still difficult to catch, partly because they are very alert by nature, but also because of their aggression. They can attack with little provocation, especially when their young are around. Some species will attack in packs of up to 15, and will make every effort to injure or even kill an intruder. They charge with considerable force, delivering a powerful head-butt that can break human bones. Some wild pigs have tusks, which they can use as slashing weapons. Thanks to these effective

defences, and the fact that some pigs are over 7ft (2.1m) in length, an encounter can be fatal for the hunter. Use spear traps and deadfalls, and never get too close.

REPTILES

Reptiles are few and far between in the temperate world, mainly because they can only maintain their body temperature through external heat sources. Consequently, most reptiles are confined to regions with temperatures in the region of 86–104°F (30–40°C). Reptiles lay eggs, which can be a useful source of nutrition. Most reptiles do not pose a threat to human beings, with the obvious exceptions of some snakes and a few of the very large lizard species, such as the gila monster and the komodo dragon. Though small, reptiles are very fast, and are equipped with sharp eyesight and a highly developed sense of smell. Catching one, therefore, takes some cunning. For the survivor in temperate climates, there are several types of reptile that can be eaten.

Lizards

Lizards are superbly adaptable creatures, and as a result they can be found in almost every type of environment except those with arctic conditions. In temperate regions, most lizards are very small – the common viviparous lizard grows to about 4.75in (12cm),

Preparing birds

Birds have to be bled like any other creature, which is done by stretching the neck and slitting it just below the tongue. Once the bird has bled fully, it requires plucking. For birds other than water-dwelling birds, dunking the creature in hot water makes the feathers easier to remove. Pluck the feathers out of the skin with sharp tugs, beginning at the chest. (N.B. Cooking the bird using the mud-cooking method will remove the feathers for you.)

Gutting birds requires an incision down from the neck to the tail; the innards can then be drawn out by hand. Once the bird is prepared, it can be cooked by boiling (for old birds or carrion birds) or roasting (for young birds).

including tail – but several together make a tasty and wholesome meal. Look for lizards basking in the sun on rocks or branches, and approach very stealthily from the rear. Try to grab them by the tail before they can flee, and kill with a swift flick or blow to the head. Alternatively, try to strike them with a long, whip-like stick.

Snakes

Snakes can pose a big problem for the survivor because some are very dangerous indeed, ranking amongst the world's most poisonous creatures. Despite this, they make an excellent meal. Before heading off on any expedition, study snake species carefully, making sure that you are able to identify the worst culprits with ease. Almost all of these are confined to desert and tropical regions, though poisonous adders are common throughout temperate North America and Eurasia (their bite, though, is rarely fatal). Even if you can identify a snake as harmless, proceed with caution, as many can give you a nasty bite. Beware of snakes playing dead – they will attack as you try to pick them up.

Kill a snake by pinning it to the ground with a forked stick just behind its head, and then striking the head several times with a heavy stick. Skin the snake by cutting off the head (from well below the poison sacks) and making a vent up to the neck to empty out the innards. Then skewer the snake at the neck and peel the skin off towards the tail. The snake can then be cut into steaks and cooked.

Turtles

Turtles and tortoises are amongst the oldest living creatures on the planet, their origins dating back some 200 million years. In that time, they have undergone only minor evolutionary adjustments. There are actually no tortoises living in temperate regions except for domesticated pets, but there are plenty of turtles, including the green turtle, loggerhead turtle and European pond turtle.

Though turtles are aquatic animals, they all lay eggs on dry land – thus the mating season or period is a good time for hunting them along sandy coastlines (turtle eggs themselves are excellent survival food). Reproductive periods can occur very frequently. The green turtle, for instance, lays over 100 eggs every two weeks, so it makes regular and dependable appearances. To kill a turtle, simply flip it over onto its back to render it helpless, then strike its head. Be careful of the jaws – most turtles have astonishingly strong bites, and some can even inject poison. Therefore, cut off the turtle's head and neck before eating it. Gut it by slicing through the belly flesh and emptying out the contents. Boiling is the best method of cooking, but watch how much you eat, because turtle meat is very rich and can lead to upset stomachs when consumed in large quantities.

AMPHIBIANS

Amphibians are divided into three basic types of creature: frogs, toads, and newts and salamanders. All three are found throughout the temperate world. Most alternate between land and freshwater lakes or ponds.

Toads are inedible because they secrete poison from under the skin, and some salamanders and newts also emit unpleasant substances to reduce the likelihood of their being eaten. Nevertheless, there are many edible species of frogs, newts and salamanders. Look for them along the banks of rivers, pond and streams. Frogs tend to come out at night, and can be located by following the sound of their croaking. A bright light will dazzle them into stillness long enough for you to kill with a blow from a stick. Gut them by pinching the belly skin in the fingers and then slicing through it. The abdominal contents can then be carefully emptied out. Cook according to whatever means you

Game birds

Game birds are most commonly killed on the wing with a shotgun. The targeted bird should be followed at first with the gun barrel, but the shot is then aimed just in front of the bird's beak to allow for the distance the bird will travel while the shot is in flight.

Whooper swan

Canada goose

Gadwell

Mallard

Teal

Snail

rous birds attracted to plants bearing fruit and seeds, make a crude model of an owl from mud and stick it on a tree. This will bring them into the open, and they will mob the 'owl', believing that they are under threat. When any bird is caught alive, kill it with a quick pull and twist of the neck.

have available – roasting is the best – and remember to savour the legs of frogs, which are regarded as a delicacy. (N.B. In the tropics, highly coloured frogs should always be avoided; some have lethally poisonous skins.)

BIRDS

Almost all species of birds, with a few notable exceptions, can fly. This ability, combined with lightning reflexes, presents a challenge to the survivor on the hunt for his next meal. With practice, projectile weapons such as catapults can be an effective way of knocking a bird off its perch. Thin netting or wire stretched between trees on known flying routes is also a good way of catching or injuring birds in flight. Baited hooks and snares also work.

The terrain you find yourself in, and the tools at your disposal, will very much determine the type of birds worth hunting. Game birds such as pheasants, partridges, ducks and geese are the most desirable because of the quality of their meat. These birds tend to inhabit thickets and dense grasses, and may have to be flushed out before you can take a shot. However, the easiest birds to catch are birds of prey and carrion birds, mainly because the hunter can easily exploit their attraction to meat. One carcass baited with several hooks should suffice. To catch smaller, herbivo-

INVERTEBRATES

Invertebrates are animals without a backbone, and are so populous that they make up more than 97 per cent of the species on this planet. They include all insect species, molluscs, crustaceans, crabs and many other perfectly edible animals. Because of their appearance, and because they are often regarded simply as a nuisance, many people find the thought of eating insects unappetizing. But most invertebrates are highly nutritious, and are delicious when cooked and prepared properly.

Slugs and snails

Look for slugs and snails around dawn when they are comfortable in the dew-laden environment. They should not be eaten as soon as they are gathered. Either starve them or restrict their diet to healthy green vegetation for about 24 hours. This

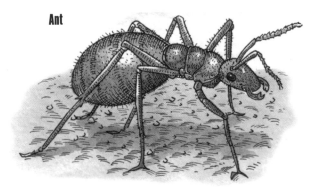

Ant

Grasshopper

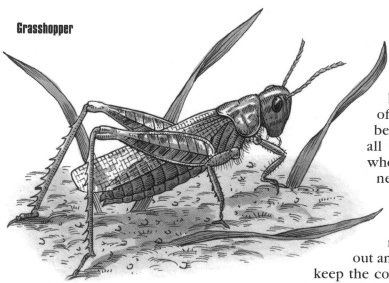

induces them to excrete their internal poisons. Once they have done so, drop them live into boiling water and cook for 10 minutes. Slugs are also good roasted. (N.B. Avoid any snails with brightly coloured shells – they are usually poisonous.)

Worms

Worms are exceptionally rich in protein and amino acids. Gather them by digging up a patch of moist earth and breaking the soil apart. To clean them out, either starve them like snails for 24 hours or squeeze them from top to bottom like a tube of toothpaste. They can then be fried, roasted or boiled. One way of getting the nutritional benefit from a worm if you find their appearance too repellent is to dry them out on a hot stone and then grind them into a powder, which can be added to another food.

Bees and wasps

While bees and wasps are edible in themselves, they also provide other foods, including pupae and larvae and, best of all, honey. The obvious obstacle to gathering these foods is that bees and wasps are stinging creatures that will attack in their hundreds if threatened, with possibly fatal results. A nest of bees or wasps can be neutralized by placing a torch or bundle of heavily smoking grass beneath it; the smoke will kill all the bees. Do this at night when all the bees will be in the nest – during the day, you might suddenly find yourself assaulted by returning worker bees. Once the nest has been smoked, drain out any honey from the combs, but keep the combs themselves as they provide a useful wax for waterproofing. Honey is a valuable find because it will keep for years and gives a powerful energy boost when needed. When eating bees themselves, remember to remove the wings, legs and poison sting and sack before cooking by boiling or roasting.

Bees' nests tend to be found in hollow structures such as old trees and caves, while wasps tend to hang their nests from branches. Never tackle a hornets' nest. The sting from these insects has a sickening impact, and 20 stings can be fatal.

Crickets and grasshoppers

These are less easy to find in temperate areas than in desert and tropical regions, where locusts are also in vast supply. They are not an especially appetizing survival food, but they are easy to kill – simply swat them with a leafy branch – and equally easy to cook. Pull off the wings, antennae and legs, and then roast.

FISH

Fish are a lifeline food for anyone attempting to survive along a river or coastal district. About 25,000 species of fish inhabit the world's waters, and many provide high pro-

Freshwater fish

The trout and bream demand different methods of catching. Trout trawl the river bed looking for food but also chase surface insects, a habit which can be exploited by a fisherman using bright lures. Bream tend to hide around rocks in slow-flowing or stagnant waters, and are best fished by a slow-moving line floated underwater.

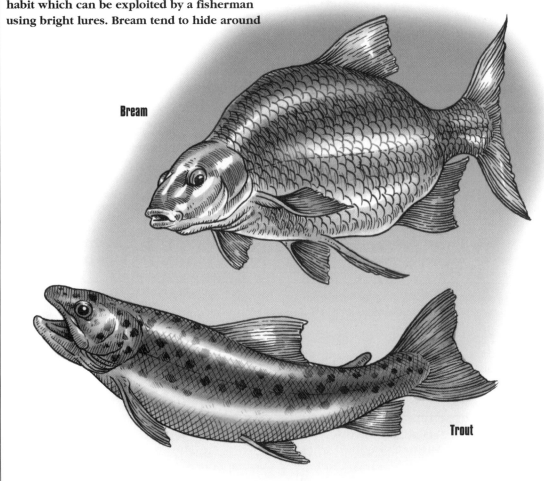

Bream

Trout

tein value, health-giving oils and essential amino acids. Having caught a fish, you must prepare it for cooking.

Any fish less than 6in (15cm) should simply be cooked whole after gutting – including the heads and tails – as they are too small to cut down. With larger fish, such as trout, scrape off the scales by running a sharp knife along the body, starting at the tail and working up towards the head. Then cut off the tail and the head at the gills. Next, lay the fish on its side and slice along the belly from the top to the bottom. Open up the fish, remove its internal organs and then wash the fish thoroughly to remove any remnants of the innards. Filleting is the most professional

Gutting and preparing a fish

Filleting a fish requires a good, sharp filleting knife; attempting to fillet with any other knife will often leave good meat behind on the bones. Firstly, prepare the fish as usual. Scrape the scales off, running the knife repeatedly from the tail to the head (A), then slice the fish open from the anus to the neck (B). Scoop out the internal organs (C). Then slowly open the fish out while pris-ing the ribs away from the flesh with the knife (D). Repeat this on the other half of the ribcage and the entire skeleton can be lifted away from the meat (E).

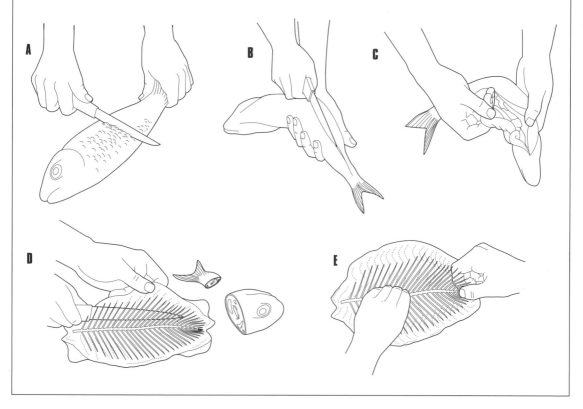

way of preparing a fish (see illustration), but without proper knives and some training this is very difficult and can be wasteful of good meat. A simple way to ensure that nothing is wasted is by simply roasting the fish whole over a fire and then flaking the meat off the bones when cooked.

Eels are more difficult to prepare. First gut the eel like a normal fish. Then drive a strong stick through the gills and suspend the eel between two supports (possibly two forked sticks). Hold the eel with a cloth to prevent slipping, and then cut around its body just beneath the head, slicing through the top layer of skin. Peel away the skin from the flesh at this joint and then, using both hands, draw the skin downward in a single peeling action. Once this is done, cut off the head and the tip of the tail. To fillet the eel, lay it down on a flat surface and run a sharp

The benefits of hanging meat

Hanging improves the texture and tenderness of meat. It is not always possible in a survival situation because there are too many health hazards, but it is recommended for tough meats where possible. In mild climatic conditions, you should hang up the gutted carcass for up to three days, allowing the acids of decomposition to tenderize tough meat fibres (do not hang offal, which should be consumed as soon as possible). Keep flies off the carcass at all times, because if they get a chance to lay their eggs, the meat will be spoiled. Also, do not hang food in very hot climates, particularly the tropics. It will detioriate significantly in just a few hours in high humidity.

knife along the backbone, parallel with the horizontal surface. Do not cut through its ribs. If done properly, this technique should leave eel fillets ready for cooking.

PREPARING MEAT

While fish are relatively simple creatures to butcher, mammals take a little more skill. The animals you are most likely to have to prepare are four-legged mammals such as sheep, deer or rabbits.

Animal foods usually require bleeding, skinning, gutting and jointing before they are ready to go on the fire. With mammals, bleeding is simple: hang the animal up by its back legs (tie around the hock, not the ankle), with the neck hanging down over a vessel to catch the blood. Slice into the throat either side of the windpipe and just behind the ears. This should sever the jugular or carotid arteries in the neck, resulting in the animal's blood draining out into the receptacle. Save the blood – it contains important vitamins, minerals and salt, and can be added to soups and stews to make them more nutritious.

Once the animal is thoroughly bled, it requires skinning, preferably while it is still warm. Place the animal on its back and cut the skin from the top of the breastbone to the anus in one long slice. Be careful – you should only slice through the surface of the skin. Do not cut any deeper or you may rupture internal organs that can pollute the rest of the meat with their contents. Take away the testicles of male animals, and also remove the anal glands of dogs and cats by carefully cutting around them. Now peel back the opening to reveal the innards. Remove them carefully, keeping the heart, liver and kidneys for later. Cut off the intestines as far up the chest cavity as possible and remove all the inner organs. Next, cut off the legs at the first joint. You should now be able to roll the skin off the animal, starting with each leg. If you have problems getting started, then make another incision down the inside of each leg from the groin/chest to the stump, folding the skin back like the spread of a book. (Be careful when doing this on deer, as some have a scent gland located just behind the knee that is unpleasant if ruptured onto the surrounding meat. Remove these by cutting around them.) The skin around the chest can usually be prized off by running your hands down inside the chest cavity between the ribs and the skin. Your goal is to turn the skin inside out from the back end of the animal and draw it off over the body and head.

The one exception to the procedure outlined above is pigs. Pigs cannot be skinned. The first priority is to remove the pig's layer of thick abrasive hairs. This is done by placing the carcass over a fire and then scraping off the singed hairs with a knife. Immersing the body in hot water (not boiling, just very hot to the touch) will also help loosen the hairs. Then butcher.

Once gutting is completed, the animal needs jointing. If you already have some experience in butchery, you will be able to separate the meat into identifiable joints. However, many people do not possess these skills, so basically split the animal at any natural joint, make steaks out of thick muscular sections of meat, and then chop up the rest of the meat in any way that looks appealing or which fits easily into your cooking vessel.

Waste nothing obtained from the process of butchering. The heart, kidneys and liver are common foods, but most offal that is cleaned thoroughly can then be boiled and eaten (stick to boiling for offal as it is the most effective way of getting rid of any internal parasites). Tough items such as the feet and tail can make an excellent base for soups and stews (be sure to clean them very diligently to remove traces of dirt and excrement), and even the heads of large animals yield nutritious meals in the tongue or cheeks. Bones have various uses as mentioned earlier, but bone marrow can be used for healthy stocks and soups simply by boiling the bones.

CHAPTER FIVE

Hunting and trapping

Most wild animals have developed superb senses for surviving the advances of predators. Hunting such creatures is often frustrating for the novice hunter, but a little practice and the correct weapons will soon result in kills.

Of all the ancient food-gathering skills rendered near obsolete by the modern world, none has been hit as hard as hunting. Hunting is a unique and demanding pursuit. It requires a surprising range of talents: stealth, physical and mental control, great patience, knowledge of the natural world, a good memory and a keen eye for detail. The survivor must learn these skills anew.

Please note, however, that the practice of hunting and trapping is heavily circumscribed by law in most countries. Find out what is permissible and what is not in your country, state or locale and obey any legislation diligently. Furthermore, the development of hunting skills calls for a deep sensitivity to the natural world. It is no coincidence that the few hunter-gatherer peoples left on the earth have a very profound respect for the creatures they hunt and the world they live in. They only hunt those creatures that they intend to eat or turn into clothing (usually both), and never kill animals just for the sheer satisfaction of watching them drop dead. They are also careful to leave enough members of any one species alive to ensure the species does not die out.

When simply practising stalking techniques to observe an animal and find out as much as possible about its behaviour and instincts, there is no need to kill it. Kill only in a real survival situation when you need to.

WEAPONS

Hunting and trapping are basically the active and passive forms of catching animal food in the wild. Hunting requires the physical pursuit of quarry by the survivor, systematically tracking down prey and moving into striking range. Trapping necessitates the same diligence in pursuit, but the method of killing is an effective trap, set and then left by the hunter.

To hunt successfully, the hunter must possess weapons that can deliver a killing blow.

Firearms

The advantages of firearms are fairly obvious. A trained shooter with an appropriate weapon can kill prey at distances reaching up to hundreds of feet (metres), which reduces the amount of time he will have to spend stalking an animal. Guns also offer superior targeting. A competent hunter should be able to achieve a group of shots in a 3in (7.6cm) diameter circle at 304ft–608ft (100–200 metres). Combine this accuracy with the takedown force of high-power rounds, and the hunt is more likely to result in a clean and humane kill (depending on where the shot is placed). Also, pulling a trigger requires negligible effort – though the stalk may be exhausting – and the return for each shot fired should be significantly higher than can be achieved with any other weapon.

The disadvantages of firearms are relatively few. They are far more dangerous than hand-launched weapons – a significant portion of the annual 40,000 plus deaths from guns in the US are the result of hunting accidents. The noise made by firearms scares off other, potential prey. Finally, the wrong type of ammunition or weapon can easily render

Types of hunting ammunition

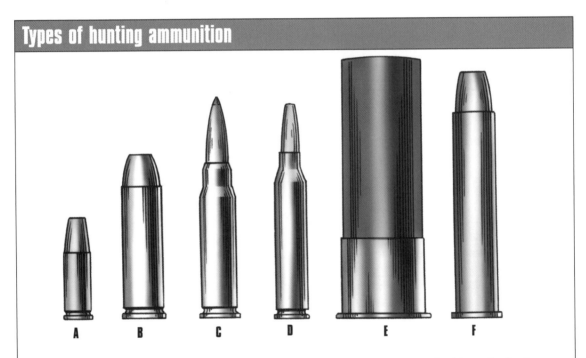

A   B   C   D   E   F

The cartridges illustrated are a typical selection of popular ammunition types. They are: 9mm pistol (A), .44 Magnum pistol (B), 7.62mm rifle (C); 5.56mm rifle (D); 12-gauge shotgun (E); and .50 rifle (F). Only the last four types are really suitable for hunting, though .44 Magnum rounds are used in some hunting handguns.

your kill inedible through the extent of the damage inflicted.

The basic guns available to a hunter are handguns, shotguns, rifles and combination guns.

Handguns

Handguns, whether revolvers, which feed the bullets from a rotating cylinder operated by the trigger, or automatics, which feed the bullets from a magazine with a reloading capacity powered by recoil, are generally unsuitable for hunting. Some companies currently manufacture powerful .44 magnum revolvers with extended barrels and even telescopic sights for big-game hunting, but most authorities advise against their use. Handguns are difficult to shoot with any accuracy over 22 yards (20m) – even less in most cases – and so cannot ensure a clean and effective kill. If you do hunt with handguns, limit your prey to animals that are more easily approached so that you can come well within range. Fire using a proper technique: extend the grip arm fully, brace the gun with both hands and take time to place the shot. Never snap shoot from the hip or with one hand, as these are good ways to wound or kill yourself or others.

Shotguns

A good shotgun is probably the best firearm for multipurpose hunting. The most common form is a double-barrelled configuration, either over-and-under or side-by-side in layout. These guns hold two cartridges when loaded. By contrast, pump-action shotguns are single-barrelled and feed cartridges in from a long tube underneath the barrel. In some models of this type, the tube can hold up to seven cartridges. Each cartridge is loaded by pumping a slide with the front hand.

Shotguns can fire specially designed single slugs, which are usually used for big-game hunting, but they most commonly shoot a spray of lead, steel, zinc, bismuth or tin shot, which spreads out as it travels. Spreading shot is more likely to hit a target than a single round. However, the further away from the prey that the shot is taken, the greater the likelihood that the animal will be peppered rather than decisively taken down. So, you should always aim to fire within 110 yards (100m), and preferably closer to 55 yards (50m).

Select gun and ammunition wisely. A 12-bore shotgun is the most popular, with pellet size numbered on a scale of 1–9. Shot size #1 is the largest at 4mm in diameter, and cartridges full of this are good for hunting larger creatures such as geese and foxes. Size #6, 2.7mm in diameter, is a sound, general-purpose shot capable of efficiently killing pigeon, pheasant, rabbit, duck and hare. Shot #9, only 2mm in diameter, is only suitable for clay pigeon shooting. Take advice from a competent gunseller before buying either a shotgun or ammunition, and be specific about intended prey. Despite large slugs being available, shotguns are really only suitable for hunting birds and smaller mammals up to the size of a fox. For anything bigger, you will need a rifle.

Rifles

The most common type of hunting weapon is a bolt-action rifle with a calibre of 7.62mm or .30in. Many higher and lower calibres are available, from .22 long cartridge rifles at the bottom (suitable for shooting foxes at most) all the way up to .50in monsters at the top with ranges of over 1641 yards (1500m) and capable of taking down an elephant. Again, take advice from your gunshop owner about the correct type of weapon for your needs. In the UK, the minimum legal requirement for a deer-shooting weapon is a .240in bullet of 100 grains in weight (50 grains for a roe deer) and with a muzzle velocity of 2450fps (feet per second). This calibre acts as a good guide for rifle purchases.

Choosing a hunting gun

Illustrated here are the three most common types of hunting gun. The 7.62mm sniper rifle has an effective range of up to 2439ft (800m). The pump-action and the double-barrelled shotgun can fire a range of ammunition types from fine shot to heavy slugs, but effective range with these weapons is limited to around 304–608ft (100–200m).

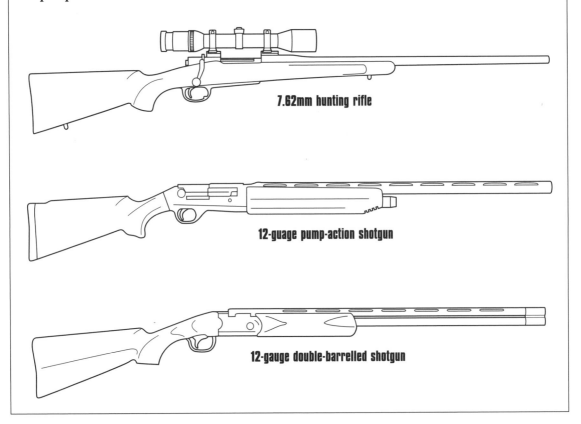

7.62mm hunting rifle

12-guage pump-action shotgun

12-gauge double-barrelled shotgun

Rifles are undoubtedly the best method of killing large game. They can be fitted with advanced telescopic sights that can be used to track and fire upon prey at distances impossible for the naked eye. However, the power of your gun makes it unsuitable for smaller game. High-velocity rounds create large, temporary cavities in their victims as the shock waves expand outward. One well-placed shot and a deer will fall down dead; hit a rabbit, and it is more likely to evaporate into fluff and fragments of bone.

Combination guns
An alternative to a rifle or a shotgun is to combine both in what are known as, quite logically, combination guns. Like shotguns, these are usually double-barrelled, though one barrel fires shotgun rounds while the other is rifled for bullets. Combination guns are not very common, though their flexibility makes them very useful survival weapons.

IN THE FIELD
Whatever the gun used, there are three prin-

Shot placement on a deer

When shooting deer, there are three main target areas which ensure a clean and quick kill. Targeting along the back of the neck (A) and the top section of the back (C) can shatter the spinal column for an instant kill, or aiming just above the shoulder (B) targets the heart and other vital organs.

explosions, make sure the end of the barrel is free of dirt or other obstructions. Carry the gun safely when walking and never rest a finger on the trigger until you are about to pull it. Pay attention also to where your bullet will fly should you miss your prey or if it goes straight through – good hunters will usually position themselves so that there is solid earth just behind their target.

Targeting

With smaller creatures like birds or rabbits, and when using a shotgun, targeting simply involves framing the whole body of the animal at the end of the barrel to ensure a hit. With big game, more sophistication is required. Resist the temptation to go for a head shot because, often, this simply results in smashing the animal's jaw or skull without entering the brain cavity. Instead, to hit the spine, aim for the top of the neck or the back, or, to hit the heart and lungs, the rib area just behind the shoulder.

ciples to shooting in the field: safety, targeting and technique.

Safety

Safety is paramount when using any firearm. Load a weapon only when about to shoot, and don't release the safety until you are actually about to pull the trigger. When resting or concluding the day's hunt, unload the gun. When you start a hunt, in order to avoid

Technique

In shooting, technique enables you to shoot well, and you can only learn to shoot properly through practice. To get instruction from experts, join a professional gun club, if at all possible. When snap shooting, ensure that the weapon is firmly in your shoulder and follow the prey smoothly with the barrel for some distance before firing. Should you be required to take another shot immediately after the first, lean into the gun slightly to aid your balance. With a long-distance rifle shot, adopt a comfortable position, with the rifle resting, if possible, on a solid object for stability. Breathe in deeply and then breathe out slowly before coming to a natural stop at the end of the breath. At this still point, the body stabilises itself. A few seconds later, when your blood is depleted of oxygen, your hold will start to wobble. It is at this still point that you should pull the trigger. (N.B. The precision gained through technique can be undone by a weapon that is not accurate, so sight your gun regularly. Shots should fall within a maximum 3in (7.6cm) radius around your point of aim).

Most of the time, however, those who find themselves suddenly cut off in a wilderness are unlikely to possess a firearm. Instead, they have to fall back on weapons made from nature.

Making a bow and arrow

Making a bow takes practice and requires basic cutting tools. Once the right piece of wood is found it is shaped (A) and then notched at each end to take the bowstring (B and C). The overall strength of the bow can be improved by gluing a stretched and scraped animal hide onto it. A bow and arrow will greatly improve your rate of success when hunting.

A

B

C

Bow and arrow

A bow and arrow is the most advanced improvised weapon. To construct the bow, first find suitable wood. Professional wooden bows are made from seasoned woods, but unseasoned materials are the more likely option in the wild. These will not hold their tension for long, so make a new bow when you notice that its performance dips. Also, to prolong the bow's life, release the pressure of the string when the bow is not in use. The types of wood that can be used include willow, hickory, oak, elm, birch and yew.

Find a flexible piece of wood about 4ft (1.2m) long and shape it with your knife so that the centre section is about 2in (5cm) wide, narrowing to 0.6in (1.5cm) at the ends. Cut right-angled notches into both ends. Now take a piece of tough string or cord and tie it into the bow ends and, with the bow under tension, make sure the cord is securely positioned in the notches. You now have a rudimentary bow.

Arrows require straight shafts of wood about 2ft (60cm) long and 0.25in (6mm) wide. Smooth the branch out by cutting off any raised parts and stripping off the bark. For the arrowheads, either sharpen the end of the stick and harden it over a fire or, better still, make an arrowhead. Arrowheads can be fashioned from slivers of flint, tin, bone or glass as long as you can sharpen them to a point. To fit the arrowhead to the shaft, split the end of the shaft about 1in (2.5cm) deep and trap the base of the arrowhead in the split. Finally, tie some cord around the end of the split just below the arrowhead to tighten the grip and stop the split slipping further down the shaft.

Flights should also be fitted, as they will dramatically improve the accuracy and distance of the arrow as it travels through the air. They can be made with any stiff, flat material, such as cardboard, but birds' feathers are the best option. Take a bird's feather and split it down the middle to make two halves. Tie each half to the base of the arrow shaft with string – cut away sections of the feather for the string to sit in. Finally, in the flight end of the shaft, cut a slot for the bowstring.

When firing the newly constructed bow and arrow, keep the arm that you grip the bow with locked out in front. Locate the cord in the notch in the end of the arrow shaft, sit the arrow shaft on top of your grip hand, and then draw the string and arrow backwards across your body, smoothly bringing the arrow up to eye level. To take aim, look down the length of the arrow just as you would a shotgun barrel. To release the string, simply unfurl your fingers slowly. One safety note – watch that the string does not burn your cheek or, even worse, snag behind your ear as you release it. With practice, a novice should soon be able to hit relatively small targets over a 66ft (20m) range.

Bola missile

The bola is an ancient weapon that can be used to bring down flying birds or to trip running animals. Take about three to six stones, each about 2in (6cm) across, and wrap them in a small piece of material (alternatively, fill pouches of material with sand). Tie a length of string about 3ft (90cm) in length to each stone-holding pouch. Complete the weapon by gathering all the ends of the strings and knotting them together very firmly. To launch the weapon, grip the knotted ends and swing the whole bola above your head before releasing it against your prey. Get used to throwing the bola after only one or two revolutions – a bola swinging for too long will alert the prey to your presence.

Slingshot

The slingshot is one of the simplest projectile weapons, yet, with practice, it can deliver a stone to a target with surprising speed and accuracy. Take a length of string or cord about 4ft (120cm) long and place a patch of

Bola missiles

The bola missile, with its multi-pronged method of attack, is ideal for bringing down running prey such as rabbits, foxes and even small deer. But remember to have a backup weapon, such as a spear, at the ready – bolas missiles will often take down and injure the prey but not kill it. You will need a back-up weapon to finish the kill.

Slingshot

With proper construction and use the slingshot is capable of accurate fire at ranges of 152ft (50m), though it is most effective as a killing weapon at about 30–76ft (10–25m). Range is increased by throwing the entire body weight into the cast and by increasing the size and speed of the spin.

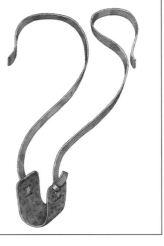

leather or cloth in the centre. Now hold both ends of the string in one hand and place a smooth stone in the pouch. To fire, rotate the sling rapidly above your head, the plane of the circle lining up with your target. Let go of one end of the string as the stone comes around in line with the target and the stone will be sent flying. Loading several small pebbles at once will produce a shotgun-type effect.

Catapult

Most schoolboys know how to make a catapult. Take a thick and solid forked twig (a fairly flexible wood such as hazel is the best) and a piece of elasticated material such as a section of the inner tube of a tyre, surgical tubing or, at worst, the elastic from your clothes. Fit a pouch to the centre of the elastic and then tie the ends of the elastic to the y-shaped fork of the branch. Stones can then be fired from the catapult simply by loading them into the pouch, pulling back the elastic and letting go. When aiming a catapult, do not attempt to look down the elastic but instead get used to targeting through regular practice. The catapult is excellent against perched birds, rabbits and small creatures.

Spear

Spears are constructed in much the same way as

Spear and spear thrower

To use a spear-thrower accurately hold the launcher by the side of the head and aim the spear at the target. Take two or three steps forward and then bring the spear launcher straight through, still pointing at the target. As the throwing arm reaches its full extension, whip the launcher downwards to release the spear.

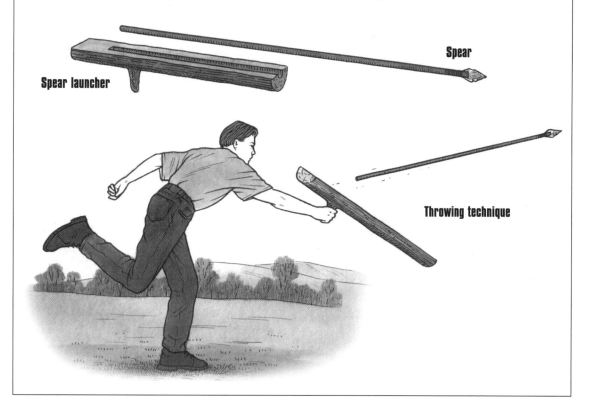

Spear

Spear launcher

Throwing technique

arrows, with the difference that all the dimensions are greater. A throwing spear should be about 3ft (90cm) long; for a spear intended only for stabbing, the dimensions can be double this. When throwing a spear, put your full body weight into the cast and follow right through with the throwing arm. You can improve the distance and accuracy of the throw by making a spear launcher. Find a tree limb, with an attached branch, about twice the width of your spear. Cut the limb down to about three-quarters of the length of your spear, and then split this limb straight down the middle. Cut a channel on the inside of the split limb that the spear can sit in snugly but without gripping the shaft. Next, cut down the branch attached to the limb so that it acts as a forward-sloping handle (see illustration).

Throwing objects

If making a projectile weapon is beyond your means, you can always rely on simple arm power. Birds, squirrels and rabbits can be killed with a well-thrown stone or piece of wood. Choose smooth stones that aren't too heavy for you and which sit easily in your hand – you need to deliver speed, not weight. Hurl several stones at once to increase your chances of hitting birds. Sticks can be useful when trying to bring down rabbits and squirrels. Skim the stick towards the target on a horizontal plane; as the wood turns, it should cut your prey down like a scythe.

HUNTING TECHNIQUES

Hunting almost always begins with the act of tracking. Tracking is the pursuit of quarry using the signs of its presence as a guide to its location. Every good tracker relies on his senses. In urban environments, where social and verbal skills are more in demand and threats to existence minimal, the senses are often underused.

Sight, for example, tends to become 'tunnelled', taking in only what the person is directly focused upon. By contrast, studies of hunter-gatherer peoples show that they use their peripheral vision far more, developing what some North American tribes call 'eagle vision'. This type of sight, which takes in the entire landscape in a 180° sweep, is ideal for hunting.

When out walking, use your senses as much as possible in order to refine them. Notice everything about your surroundings: colours, noises, smells, sensations, tastes in the air – truly 'stare' with the senses. Don't let your attention wander for a moment, but absorb every scrap of information about the surrounding world, without judging or evaluating it. (People practising this for the first time often discover a sense of connection with reality and the external world that they have never known before.)

In hunting, however, heightened senses need to be backed up by sound knowledge of animal characteristics and behaviour patterns. Before attempting to hunt any animal, you should aquaint yourself thoroughly with the following information:

- What the animal eats and where these food sources are.
- Feeding patterns and signs that feeding has taken place.
- The type of environment the animal inhabits.
- The times of day or night when the animal is active.
- The times of year when the animal's young will be present.
- What the animal's footprints and droppings look like.
- What burrows, dens or nests the animal builds.
- How it might change its appearance with the seasons.
- How it moves and the limitations of its movements (e.g., can it climb trees?)
- What other animals are likely to be found in its environment.
- What creatures it is hunted by.

Build up an advanced profile of your intended quarry and, in the field, have this information firmly in your mind. It will help you to seek out the right places for hunting. Once there, you need closer tracking skills.

The meaning of sign

In professional tracking, the signs of a quarry's presence are known as 'sign'. Sign is divided into two types: ground sign and top sign, the former being anything below ankle height, the latter being anything above ankle height. Examples of these, when applied to animal tracking, are as follows:

Ground sign:
Animal runs in the grass
Burrows
Debris from dropped food
Disturbances to ground features, such as crushed molehills
Dew knocked from vegetation
Droppings
Dusting sites

A guide to mammal footprints

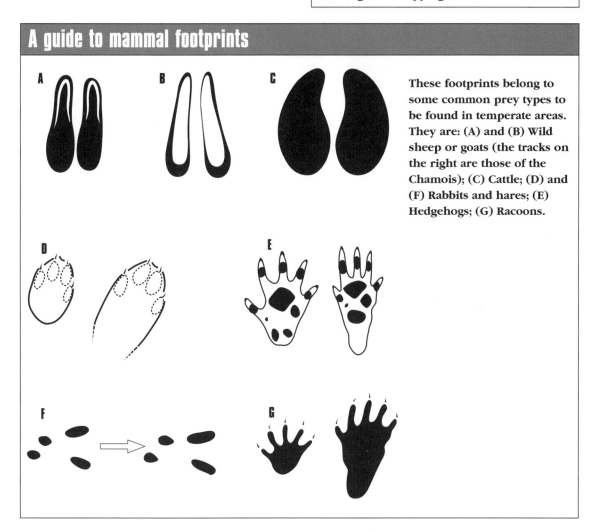

These footprints belong to some common prey types to be found in temperate areas. They are: (A) and (B) Wild sheep or goats (the tracks on the right are those of the Chamois); (C) Cattle; (D) and (F) Rabbits and hares; (E) Hedgehogs; (G) Racoons.

Footprints
Fur or feathers
Soils, mud, etc deposited by the animal

Top sign:
Broken/bent vegetation
Broken cobwebs
Chewed bark or roots
Fur or feathers caught on vegetation
Nests
Scratch marks on trees

The kinds of sign are effectively endless, but categorising sign into 'ground' and 'top' can give the tracking an initial shape. Usually, the first things to look out for are physical tracks. Check the ground carefully, looking for patches of flattened grass or, best of all, clear footprints in the soil or mud. These footprints should establish the species of the creature and the direction in which it was heading. Tracks such as these are especially valuable because animals tend to use regular routes for feeding and travel. Confirm this by checking if the tracks are overlaid with a fresh set the next day.

When following tracks, you will find that they often peter out because the conditions

How time affects sign

A competent tracker judges sign by many factors, and time is one of the most important. A clear set of tracks may be of less value if they are days old than a fresh set of tracks erratically carved in mud. Tips for judging the time of sign include:

● Usually, the more recent the paw or hoof print, the more sharply it will be defined in the ground. As time passes, water will often seep into the track and the edges will crumble. The print will also fill up with leaves, seeds, etc.

● If faeces retain any heat, then they have been passed very recently.

● Flattened grass usually becomes vertical again within three or four hours of being trampled.

● Broken parts of vegetation will start to die immediately. Observe the dying and decomposition rates of any such parts for future reference.

● Thick vegetation grown over a den may indicate that the den is no longer in use.

on the ground are not receptive to tracks. (Tracks leading through a shallow river would be one such example). When this happens, switch to top sign to continue the tracking. Look for broken twigs, particularly ones that are still green and fresh looking, because this indicates that an animal has passed by recently. Also, look to see if the animal has fed along the way – signs of feeding may imply that the particular route you have been following has come to an end. Look out for shredded or scratched bark, nibbled roots, saplings that have been bitten off, piles of discarded nut shells, pieces of fruit, signs of the ground having been dug up for food, and even signs that a violent struggle has taken place with another animal, such as churned-up earth and torn flesh or blood.

Animal droppings are also important. They can be as clear as footprints when it comes to determining what species of animal you are following. Depending on the level of freshness, droppings can also tell you how long it has been since the animal was at that spot. Fresh droppings still emitting an odour are recent, while dry droppings that don't smell are old. The first fact to be gleaned from droppings is whether a creature is a carnivore or a herbivore. Carnivorous (or omnivo-rous) animals tend to produce long stools that taper at the end, while herbivores pass more rounded dung that is usually heavily matted with the vegetation they consume. Birds that live solely on seeds, fruit and vegetation pass a fairly liquid stool, while carnivorous birds – especially those that prey mainly on lizards and mice – pass pellets that often have a dry, crumbly consistency and which may contain the bones of the creature or creatures they've eaten.

While it is easy to identify single points of sign, putting them all together to determine a course of tracking is often problematic. Stand at one piece of sign and explore methodically around it in a circle until you find a corresponding sign. Link the two together in your mind's eye. Stand on the second piece of sign and repeat the process again until you have three pieces of sign giving you a good general direction to follow. By linking one track to the next the hunter should be able to track the animal to source. However, the hunter needs to be very sensitive to erratic deviations, such as if the animal was suddenly scared, and also needs to be aware that as he closes in on the animal it may pick up his presence and actively seek to hide or escape.

Stealth

When it comes to the actual moment of hunting, stealth is the keyword. With mammals in particular, keep downwind of the creature (i.e. the wind blows from the animal towards you). Otherwise, human scent will be carried to the animal's highly developed sense of smell. Do not stand out on hills or silhouette yourself against hedges, trees, etc. Instead, plot a route towards the creature that follows natural cover. Camouflage yourself by attaching pieces of vegetation to your clothing. Make sure, though, that the plants are natural to the area (if it's a planned survival trip, don't take unsuitable camouflage with you). And don't use too much, as it will

make walking difficult and only results in the highly visible sight of a 'stalking bush'. Be silent. When walking, lift the knee high and slowly, and lower your foot straight down, making ground contact with the toe first to feel for any material that might crunch or crack underfoot. Then, slowly, roll the rest of the foot into contact with the ground. If you are getting very close to your prey, you may have to go into a crawl. Should you be spotted or heard, simply freeze and hold position until the animal resumes normal activity.

When attempting the kill, make decisive movements and use your weapon with ferocious intent – remember you are trying to kill the creature, not just hit it. If the animal

Gathering insects

To gather insects from a termite or ant nest, simply insert a long stick into the nest (A), hold it there for a few seconds to allow the insects to bite onto it, then withdraw it and scrape the insects off the stick into a container (B). Wear gloves if available to prevent insect bites.

is wounded and runs off into the bush, do not immediately follow it. Instead, wait for about five minutes to give the animal time to stop to recover. If you pursue immediately, it will just keep going. Then, track it once again, using blood as an additional sign, until you find the animal and finish it off.

The coup de grâce varies depending on the animal and the state it is in. For wounded but still dangerous animals, use your weapon again. With a badly wounded creature that is safe to touch, slit the throat deeply either side of the windpipe to despatch it. In the case of birds and small mammals, pull the head away from the body with a sharp twist to break the neck. Whatever the means, make it ruthless and efficient so as not to prolong the animal's suffering.

TRAPPING

Trapping is an alternative to hunting that some survivors might find more appealing. It involves leaving mechanisms that are triggered by the animal itself. These mechanisms either kill the animal or hold it in place until the hunter can return to finish it off. Professionally produced traps are avail-

able. These may require a trapping licence before they can be purchased, a licence that is usually only issued to legitimate fur-hunters. If you do practice trapping, make sure that you do so within the full limits of the law, because the cruelty of trapping methods can, rightly, invite severe punishment if it is undertaken without a legitimate reason.

Trapping requires very precise tracking skills. For any trap to work, it has to satisfy demanding criteria. It must be placed directly on the animal's regular route of travel – mainly feeding routes or paths taken to burrows or dens. Traps must be camouflaged as naturally as possible, using materials found in the immediate environment. The trigger mechanisms have to be sensitive enough to trip when touched by the animal, but resistant to other environmental pressures such as wind or falling leaves. They must also have the strength to restrain or incapacitate the creature swiftly and efficiently, and keep it there until you return.

Satisfying all of these criteria is not easy, but there are four basic categories, using different materials and suited to different prey,

Tracking tips

Deer
Deer often strip bark, twigs and buds. In winter, bark is chewed off in patches. In summer, it is taken off in long strips. Deer may also scratch their antlers against trees to remove their velvet. Branches or saplings trimmed off at a level height often indicate the presence of grazing deer.

Rabbits
Tend to stay close to their warrens. They are most active in the early morning and at night, though in darker climes they can remain active throughout the day. Rabbits may change fur colour in the winter.

Squirrels
Piles of discarded nutshells beneath a tree might indicate

a squirrel's nest above. Squirrels also strip patches of bark and dig up small patches of ground for shoots

Wild pigs
Root through the earth and turn over large patches of soil. They also bathe in muddy hollows. If the splashes of water over the side of the hole appear fresh, then the pig may have visited recently.

How to make a simple snare

A snare such as this is simple to construct requiring only rope or wire, and, depending on the strength of the wire, can hold prey indefinitely. However, such traps are very cruel on the snared animal and unless they are checked frequently the prey is likely to be taken by other predators which respond to the animal's distress calls.

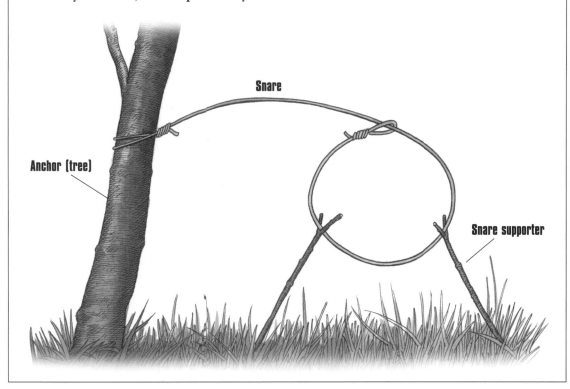

Snare

Anchor (tree)

Snare supporter

that make it slightly less difficult: snares, deadfall traps, spear traps and bird traps.

Snares

Of all the trap types, snares are the simplest and require only a piece of non-ferrous wire with a slip-loop to work. A noose is formed at the end of the wire, with the other end firmly attached to a solid object that cannot be pulled away. The noose is then positioned over an animal walkway or burrow. The principle is that the animal inadvertently puts its neck or a leg into the noose, which it draws tight around itself when it tries to walk off, either strangling itself or trapping itself there for you to find on your return.

A simple snare for catching rabbits and other small mammals can be constructed in minutes. The snare loop should be about 4in (10cm) in diameter and set about 2.5in (6cm) off the ground. It is held in that position by using two small forked twigs as braces if necessary. Set the loop over the animal trail with the other end of the snare tied to a stake or tree off the main track. Place an obstruction across the track – a thick log will do – about 5in (13cm) in front of the trap. This not only visually obscures your trap

How to make a sprung snare

The sprung snare requires more construction than the simple snare but produces better results. An animal caught in such a snare will be more quickly killed by strangulation and by suspending it high in the air it is less likely to be stolen by other predators.

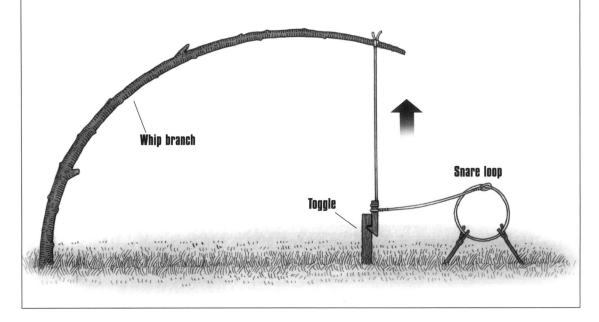

Whip branch

Toggle

Snare loop

from the animal as it comes down the track, but also forces it to hop over the obstacle straight into the snare.

This very simple snare can also be adapted for large animals, using larger dimensions and increased strength. You should be aware that it is possibly the cruellest of traps (snare use is prohibited in many countries). A snare of this type will rarely kill an animal. Instead, it will be held by the loop and exhaust and injure itself by struggling to get free. It will then either die from self-inflicted injuries or be killed when the hunter returns. Also, bear in mind that a rabbit restrained by the snare is a gift for a passing fox or other carnivore, so check the trap regularly to prevent your meal being stolen.

A solution to both of these problems is to make a spring snare. With spring snares, the end of the snare is not attached to a fixed object but to a branch held under tension. When the trap is triggered, the branch is released and actually lifts the trapped animal off the ground. Dangling off the ground, the prey is less likely to be eaten by other hunting animals and will usually die fairly quickly from strangulation.

A straightforward spring snare can be made as follows. Position the snare loop as normal, but tie the end of the snare to a small piece of wood (known as a toggle) with a right-angled lip cut into it. This lip engages with a corresponding notch in a stake that is firmly embedded in the ground. The lip and notch are only held together by tension; this tension is created by tying another piece of wire or string between the toggle and a sapling or branch bent down over the trap.

The principle of this snare is that the animal is trapped in the snare and disengages the toggle from the stake as it pulls away. This, in turn, allows the branch to spring upwards, lifting the prey off the ground.

The snares described here are the most basic of types, but there are many, many more of varying degrees of complexity. However, many advanced snares require some engineering talent to construct, and are therefore not ideal for everyone. The chances of any trap working well, however, are considerably increased by baiting the trap. Bait the trap with the kind of food eaten by the animal you are intending to catch, taking care to position the pieces so that the animal has to reach into the trap to take them. One trick with a spring snare is to tie another piece of wire between the toggle and a stick positioned over the other side of the track, with the food threaded onto the wire and positioned behind the snare. The anchor stick of this construction must be inserted quite loosely into the ground. If it is driven in hard, it may stop the tensed branch whipping upwards when the snare is tripped.

Deadfall traps

Deadfall traps kill by crushing. A heavy weight is attached, through a series of easily triggered links, to a baited release mechanism. When the bait is taken, the release mechanism allows the weight to drop directly onto the prey.

Deadfalls are mainly suitable for medium-sized mammals (foxes, badgers, pigs, etc.) and birds, but can be scaled up to impressive dimensions to kill even large game such as deer and bears. (During the Vietnam War, the Vietcong used them against US soldiers.) As with all traps, make sure when testing deadfalls that you dismantle them completely after use to prevent injury or death.

The simplest deadfall is a log propped up by a pointed stick with a protruding branch baited on the end beneath on the inside corner of the log's angle. (See Deadfall trap 1). Any animal that touches the bait disrupts the support and the log then falls down on top of it. See the illustrations in this chapter for making two very effective deadfall traps.

With deadfall traps, there are some general rules that you should follow. First, work out whether a deadfall is right for you in the

Tips for siting and setting traps

- Handle the trap as little as possible with your bare hands because animals will pick up your scent and be wary. Bury a manufactured trap in the ground for a few days to remove the smells of artificial production. Also, set you trap well away from the smells of your camp, such as woodsmoke and cooked foods.

- Don't stand or work on the animal trail you are trapping. Instead, keep to one side.
- If you have broken branches to camouflage your trap, smear mud over the white inner wood so that it does not stand out brightly against the green foliage.
- Mark your sets so that they can be found easily after a snowstorm or other heavy weather. However, make the marks some way from the actual trap (carving directional arrows onto prominent trees can be good).
- Place some bait in the intended trapping site before actually setting the trap to see if it disappears. If it does, then the location is suitable for the trap.

first place. Because deadfalls involve the setting of a weight and a release mechanism, it usually takes two people to make one. Deadfalls are also one of the more dangerous traps for the trapper, so never set the release mechanism with your body directly under the deadfall weight or the trap may claim you. There's a steep learning curve to making a deadfall trap because the release mechanisms need to be so finely balanced. Invariably, the novice trapper will make many inefficient traps before getting it right.

When baiting a deadfall, make sure that with hinge-type traps – traps where the weight is propped up between the ground and the release-mechanism, usually at a 45° angle – the bait is well back towards the hinge. This lengthens the distance the animal has to cover before it can escape the trap and increases the chances of a clean hit. Also, be sensitive to just how heavy you need to make the killing weight. A massive log will simply pulverise the meat of a small bird or rabbit.

Spear traps

Well-made spear traps have quite lethal potential, and, if proportioned correctly, will easily despatch a pig, badger or goat. Like spring snares, spear traps rely on a branch held under tension, but the method of killing is quite different. Sharpened spikes of wood are attached to the end of the branch. The

Deadfall trap (1)

This type of deadfall trap relies on multiple weights to increase the likelihood of a kill by impacting over a large area. The weights used in deadfalls can be anything which has sufficient killing force when dropped. Typical items include logs, large rocks, packs full of small stone, and large tin cans full of sand.

Support

Deadfall weights

Trigger mechanism

Bait

branch is bent back under tension and held by a release mechanism. When this mechanism is tripped, the branch is released and the spikes are catapulted into the prey.

The biggest problem with making a good spear trap is targeting. Position the bait at the point the spears will shoot through when released. Having multiple spears increases your chances of hitting the prey. To make a basic spear trap, find an animal route with a tree growing by the side. The tree should have long, whippy branches that extend over the track. (If the tree does not have appropriate

branches, then simply use a bough cut from another tree and tie it on very firmly.) Tie sharpened wooden spikes to a point on one of the branches and attach a long string or cord to the tip of the branch. Then, bend the branch back under tension around the trunk of the tree, holding it in place by taking the string around the trunk and tying the other end to a stake set in the middle of the animal track. Attach the bait to this stake. If aligned properly, the trap will release the branch when an animal tries to eat the bait, spearing the animal and, with luck, killing it outright.

Deadfall trap (2)

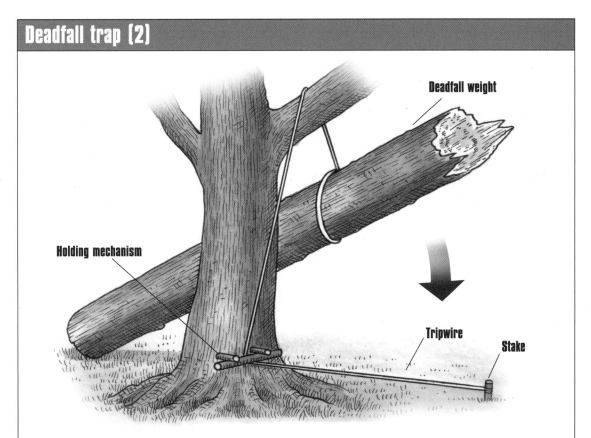

This deadfall is triggered by tripwire. The wire is tied to a stake, fed under a holding mechanism set into a tree, taken over a bough further up the tree and tied to the deadfall weight itself. When an animal hits the tripwire the holding mechanism is pulled from the tree and the log falls to the ground. The stake should pull from the ground as the weight descends.

There are many variations on the basic spear trap. The spears can hack down from above or sweep horizontally to the ground. Spears can even be attached to a deadfall trap for an added lethal edge. But with spear traps, you should always take every precaution. Remember exactly where the traps have been set and give them a very wide berth.

Bird traps

Bird traps require unique trapping mechanisms. Minor deadfalls can be used for small birds, and spear traps have their place against large birds of prey, carrion birds or game birds, but there are better ways to gather a number of birds in one go.

Rows of very fine snares, with nooses about 0.5-1in (1.5-2.5cm), made out of horsehair or fishing line, can make excellent trapping devices. Set them close together, with the nooses facing upwards, along a branch commonly used for perching. The flapping of one trapped bird may well attract others, and once two or three are caught, you can empty the trap and reset it. A line of snare can also be placed on a wire

Spear trap (1)

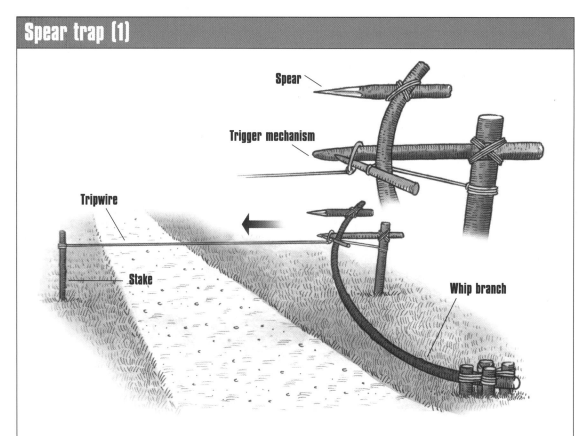

This spear trap is of simple construction, though the release mechanism may take practice to perfect. The important point is to align the sweep of the spear when it is released with the positioning of the tripwire, otherwise the spear is likely to miss the prey. Do not over bend the whip branch as the flight path of the spear will be more erratic when released.

Spear trap (2)

Here the whip branch is held by two short sticks fitted through a slip ring. The slip ring is made of any smooth material such as bound creeper, leather or any other material which will not snag on the sticks. When an animal moves the tripwire, the toggle on the end of the tripwire pulls away the slip ring and the spear is released.

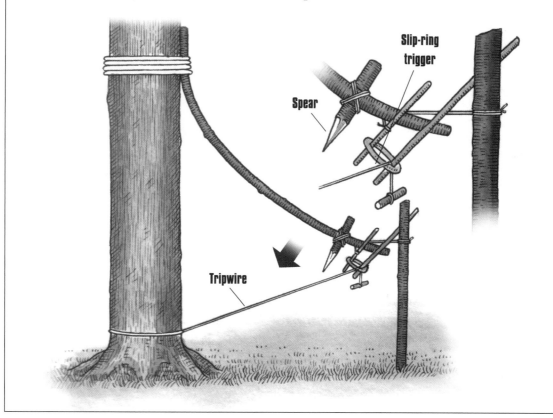

hung just above a stream to catch water-skimming birds.

Another method of catching perching birds is birdlime. Birdlime can be made by the traditional method of boiling holly leaves and starchy grain in water, and reducing the fluid until only a viscous, glue-like substance remains. Spread this substance onto prominent branches. Any birds that land on the lime will be held fast.

To catch flying birds requires either a net or a number of fine wires strung between trees on common flight paths. Nets will snare and hold the birds when they fly into them. The wires will injure or kill the birds, which can then be collected off the ground. If you have gathered a number of dead birds, never stack them in piles, because the remaining body heat will accelerate decomposition.

CHAPTER SIX

Making fire and cooking

The efforts of hunting and foraging will be wasted if foodstuffs are ruined through improper cooking techniques. Survival cooking is fundamentally concerned with making food safe and nutritious to eat.

Cooking wild foods is an essential survival activity. Learning how to get a fire going and cook on it will help the digestive system cope with strange and unfamiliar substances taken straight from nature – not just meat, but many vegetables as well. Thorough heating destroys most of the bacteria, germs, worms and flukes that infect food, and can also neutralize the stinging properties of plants such as nettles. Heat and smoke from the fire can also be used for food preservation.

THE ELEMENTS OF FIRE

All fires (apart from artificial gas fires) require three elements if they are to be successful – tinder, kindling and fuel. If any of these elements is lacking or inadequate, then the fire will fail, and valuable energy will be wasted building it. A successful fire also calls for plentiful supplies of air. Without air, no fire, regardless of the fuel being used, will burn effectively, and is more likely to go out. Note: the air intake can be varied to produce different qualities of fire, from a blazing bonfire to a smouldering low heat. Introduce more air, either by stoking the fire or channelling a draught, and the temperature of the fire will be raised, consuming more fuel. Restrict the amount of air, and the opposite happens.

Tinder

Tinder is the vital ingredient for making fire. It has to ignite easily, even after just a few sparks. Therefore, tinder is best made up of small pieces of light, dry materials. In the wild, the main sources of tinder are:

Bark and wood

Many woods and barks make excellent tinder if very dry and shredded into small, easily combustible flakes. Birch and cedar barks are particularly good thanks to their resinous content, which quickly catches light. If using wood, dead logs are good because decay will have already begun the process of breaking down the plant fibres. When wood is wet, dig deep inside because, in thick logs, the inner fibres may well be dry. Also, look at where insects have burrowed into trees – the route of their journey is often covered with sawdust, another good tinder.

Birds' nests

The insides of birds' nests are usually covered with small particles of dry grasses and soft, downy feathers. These two materials combined make excellent tinder.

Cotton and linen

Cotton and linen can be 'converted' into tinder by lightly scorching the fabric and then breaking up the fibres. Also, look for bits of cotton fluff gathered in the pockets of trousers, coats, etc.

Fungi

Almost all fungi can be turned into tinder by drying pieces and then powdering them into flaky particles. Bracket fungi – fungi that cling to trees – are excellent for tinder in that their soft interiors are often bone dry thanks to a tough, waterproof outer skin.

Grasses

Tall grasses can be made into a combustible bundle for tinder. Split and fray the grass as much as possible to provide fine fibres that will easily catch light.

Leaves

Choose dead, dry leaves and crumble them up into fine pieces.

Moss

Dry the moss out by placing it on a dry rock under the sun.

All these substances, made into a bundle about the size of two fists, can be used to ignite a fire. Tinder materials in general can be prepared in a number of ways. Perhaps the best methods are scraping and rubbing. Use a knife or sharp rock to scrape the tinder material into flakes or a powder. Or rub the material against itself or another abrasive material to break it down. Whichever method you use, all tinder must be exceptionally dry. If it is not, place it near a heat source and let it dry out slowly. Alternatively, put it in a coat or trouser pocket and let body heat do the work. Once the tinder is dry, keep it in a sealed tin or bag away from water or damp.

Kindling

Kindling is the material that is added to the tinder once it has caught fire. Kindling gives the gathering flames something more solid to feed off and raises the heat before larger pieces of fuel are added. Without good kindling on hand, a tinder fire will rapidly burn itself out.

Kindling ideally consists of small, dry twigs, usually no thicker than a pencil, but small chippings of dry wood can also serve the purpose. Like tinder, kindling must be bone dry because the heat of the tinder fire is not sufficient to dry out damp wood. When in wet surroundings, find a thick branch and cut away the outer bark and fibres until you reach the dry wood at the centre. Softwoods make valuable kindling thanks to their resinous, inflammable properties but, because they burn quickly, make sure to have ample supplies at the ready for when they're needed. Trees to avoid when selecting kindling include alder, chestnut, poplar, and willow – the wood from these trees smoulders rather than burns.

One way to improve the performance of kindling is to 'feather' the sticks. With a sharp knife, cut multiple small flaps in the surface of the branch. A branch cut like this will burn more easily than a smooth branch. Kindling needs to be added in a measured way. Don't just drop a huge pile on the burning tinder because this will simply starve the fire of oxygen and it will go out. Instead, add a branch at a time, keeping pace with the rate of ignition as the fire grows.

Fuel

The final stage of making a fire is adding fuel, without which it is no use as a source of heat or for cooking. The most obvious types of fuel are larger branches and logs. Once the kindling is blazing, don't immediately add a huge log, but gradually work your way from the smallest to the largest. This will allow the fire time to gain a proper hold. Again, at no point smother the fire with too much fuel; give it space and a chance to breathe openly.

The best woods for cooking and a steady source of heat are maple, birch, beech, hickory, oak and sycamore. These burn slowly and give off a strong heat, and, usefully, reduce to smouldering coals, which means a longer cooking time. Remember when selecting wood that each type will impart certain tangs and flavours to the food as it cooks. On the whole, avoid the more resinous woods, and opt instead for hardwoods over softwoods. Softwoods burn more quickly than hardwoods, and when roasting meat, this can have the effect of charring the outside of the flesh but leaving the inside undone. The stage at which you add fuel is also the only time when damp woods can be introduced to the fire.

Wood is only one of a long list of possible fuels. Not all are suitable for direct cooking as some give off acrid and unpleasant fumes, but they can be used to heat hotplates and stones, which in turn are useful for cooking. Optional fuels include:

Animal dung

Not the most pleasant of fire fuels, and certainly not one to cook over openly. Nevertheless, dry animal dung is perfectly usable. Cow dung is best because in its dried form, it comes in convenient 'pats' or 'chips'. Animal dung can be burnt in its natural state or mixed with wood chips, grass, etc to make a more robust and longer-burning fuel.

Coal

Coal can occasionally be found lying loose on the ground in some areas, mainly natural habitats (particularly tundra areas) in the colder parts of the Northern hemisphere. Burn as you would on a domestic fire.

Oils/petrochemicals

Combustible oils can come from several sources: from oil derived from nuts or animal fats, to oil taken from a vehicle. A vehicle can provide a number of flammable materials, including petrol and oil, antifreeze and hydraulic brake fluids, and upholstery and tyres. When using petrol (gasoline), exercise extreme caution. Untreated petrol (gasoline) tends to explode rather than burn when exposed to a naked flame, so, for survival purposes, you need to make it more stable. Mix petrol (gasoline) with sand as a retardant and burn the mixture in a pit or container as an added safety precaution. Conversely, oil and antifreeze – both substances that are very difficult to ignite – can be mixed with a small quantity of petrol (gasoline) or even potassium permanganate, which act as accelerants. With all petrochemical ignitions, ignite using a wick at a safe distance.

Peat

Peat is a combustible, soft, springy soil type found on well-drained bogs or moors. Peat has a blackened, dry appearance, and it can be cut into blocks for fuel. Stack the blocks, leaving plenty of space for ventilation.

Burning peat tends to smoulder slowly and the heat given off can be low.

This list of fuels in not exhaustive, and in a survival situation you should try to use your imagination and your senses to locate additional fuel sources. One caution when using man-made materials – beware of poisonous fumes. Certain types of material, particularly foam-type substances (such as those often found in upholstery) can give out lethal hydrogen cyanide gas when burnt, and any type of burning produces carbon monoxide, an odourless gas that can kill if inhaled in an unventilated setting. Look for fire-warning labels on any artificial fuels and also make sure that there is a plentiful supply of fresh air. The latter may not sound too difficult to

Flint-and-steel method of lighting a fire

A flint-and-steel is one of the most durable firelighting method in a survival situation. Some flint kits come with blocks of magnesium to aid ignition. Simply cut off some flakes of magnesium onto the tinder (A) then scrape the saw across the flint to direct a shower of sparks onto the tinder mix (B). Naturally occurring flint is far less reliable. Hit it with a strong downward action using the back of a knife to produce sparks (C).

achieve outdoors, but if smoke is blowing back into a shelter or getting trapped in a natural space, then there is a danger to people.

FIRELIGHTING

To recap: the basic process of survival fire-making involves igniting tinder, adding kindling and then, gradually, larger pieces of fuel, increasing the heat of combustion at each stage. There are more convenient, man-made substances that can be used at any of these stages. In terms of tinder, options include cotton wool soaked in paraffin, fire sticks (blocks of wood shavings treated with flammable chemicals) and paraffin blocks. These will ignite very easily indeed, and can save having to collect tinder from various sources. The flammable chemicals that these contain means that they can also be used when wet. Another improvised accelerant is gunpowder from ammunition – if you are carrying firearms. Draw the head out of a bullet and pour the bullet contents into your tinder pile. Then light – at a safe distance with a wick. The powder will burn fast, so make sure that you have the kindling ready to sustain the flames.

On any survival adventure, take with you copious supplies of 'strike anywhere' type matches, sealed in a waterproof container. As an extra precaution against dampness, waterproof these matches further using candle wax. Light a candle and then drip the melted wax over the match heads, allowing it to harden. This coating protects each match from the wet. When you need to use the match, simply scrape the wax off with your thumbnail. One tip: if your matches are a bit damp, rub them through your hair a few times (if your hair is not wet or too greasy). The static electricity in your hair will dry out the match.

If no matches are available, then the survivor must resort to other methods of ignition. Using a flint and steel is a classic survival technique for lighting a fire. If the tinder is of good quality, it should be possible to light it with just a few sparks. Flint is a rock that, when struck in a hard, scraping motion with a piece of steel, produces a shower of such sparks. However, natural flint is surpassed in efficiency by the man-made flint-and-steel sets available from camping and adventure stores. These usually feature a magnesium alloy 'flint' and an attached steel striker. The sparks made using this device should be more than enough to light the tinder.

Another way of lighting a fire is the classic schoolboy technique involving a magnifying glass. Turn the glass to face into the sun and concentrate the rays into a single point of light. The great heat generated at this point will soon cause the tinder to smoulder and ignite. Blowing gently on the smouldering tinder encourages the flames. Obviously, this technique is limited by the amount of sunlight available, so it is unreliable as a primary emergency firelighting strategy, especially in gloomy climes.

The methods of fire-lighting that most people will be familiar with are friction methods. These methods have been used since prehistory, and have played their part in helping mankind settle in some of the coldest regions of Earth. There are three techniques in particular: the hand drill, bow drill and fire plough.

Hand Drill

The hand-drill method is the simplest of the friction-based fire-lighting techniques. First, find a fairly large piece of softwood (pine is ideal) and cut a small V-shaped notch into the edge of the wood. At the point of the 'V', etch out a small indentation. With these modifications, this piece of wood can now act as your hearth. Your next piece of equipment is simply a hardwood stick, roughly 59in (40cm) long and about 1in (2.5cm) thick. Sharpen one end of this stick to a point.

To begin the process of fire-lighting, place a quantity of tinder beneath the V-shaped notch. Don't let the hearth sit tightly on the tinder – if necessary, create a small air gap by placing a stick beneath the edge of the hearth. Kneel on the hearth to make it secure. Next, insert the sharpened point of the stick into the indentation bored into the hearth.

Starting at the top of the stick, rotate it between your hands vigorously, letting your hands work naturally from the top of the stick to the bottom as you maintain the downward pressure. As you reach the bot-tom of the stick, stop and quickly move your hands to the starting position again and repeat. Keep repeating, maintaining speed and pressure. Friction heat builds up in the indentation and starts to produce smoke, hot ashes and coals, and sparks. The ash and coals in particular gather in the hole until they fall through the V-shaped notch and onto the tin-der, causing ignition. As soon as the tinder catches light, blow gently on it to fan the flames, and then either remove the hearth

Hand drill method of lighting a fire

Lighting a fire by hand drill is quite exhaust-ing but can take as little as one minute depending on the wood types used and the level of expertise. Note here that the person is almost leaning directly over the drill. This position helps maintain the constant and consistent pressure on the drill required to produce ignition.

Using a bow drill

The bow drill method of firelighting relies on the sound construction of the bow (A). The bow-string material is particularly important: use buckskin, belt-lacing, or a strip of pliable leather about 0.3in (0.7cm) wide. The speed of rotation should be increased at the point where the hearth begins to smoke to produce ignition (B).

and add kindling, or move the burning tinder to a fire.

The hand drill is a tiring way of making fire, and needs practice before you can get it to work efficiently. A bow drill is much faster.

Bow drill

The bow drill method of fire-lighting is, in principle and in most of its materials, identical to the hand-drill method. However, the significant difference lies in a far more efficient technique of powering the rotation of the stick in the hearth. This involves making a simple bow.

Take a strong stick about 2ft (61cm) long by 1in (2.5cm) thick. Cut two notches into the stick, one at each end. Tie a piece of strong string or cord to the stick, with the ends of the cord sitting in the notches, forming a small bow just like a bow and arrow. Leave a little slack in the cord. Next,

Fire plough method of lighting a fire

The fire plough is possibly the least efficient of the friction-based methods of fire-lighting, as the action of driving the stick backwards and forwards along the groove is slow to produce heat. Keep the plough out of the wind otherwise the flakes of tinder will cool as they are produced in the groove.

The final piece of equipment is a small, fairly thick piece of hardwood – small enough to fit comfortably in the hand. Carve a hole in the middle to receive one end of the sharpened stick. To set up the bow drill, place one tip of the stick into the hearth indentation, while pushing down on the stick from above with the hand-held piece of wood (with the other tip of the stick fitted into the carved hole). Then, applying pressure and keeping the bow at a right angle to the stick, start pushing the bow backwards and forwards in a sawing action. If the bow is made properly, this should result in the stick rotating fast – far faster – and more continuously than it would by hand power alone. Maintain this motion and the results will be the same as with the hand drill – a hot coal will build up in the hearth and ignite the tinder.

Fire plough

The fire plough is another, less well-known method of friction fire-making. This uses a fairly long piece of softwood with a carved groove about 0.7in (2cm) wide and 0.3in (1cm) deep. This groove must run the length of the board and run right off the end. Tinder is placed at the end of the groove. Friction heat is then produced by rubbing a hardwood stick vigorously up and down the groove, running from one end to the other and producing flakes of wood take your rotating stick and sharpen both ends. Carve a groove around the circumference at the stick's mid point. Then, twist the string of the bow once around the stick, in the groove.

tinder in the groove. As the heat builds up, the tinder ignites and is pushed forward by the action of the stick to drop onto the main tinder at the end of the groove.

These methods of firelighting are notoriously difficult for the unpractised, but persist in them because their effectiveness has been proved time and again. If they don't seem to be working, consider every element in turn to see if that's where the fault lies, especially the quality of the tinder, the tinder's exposure to the air, and the types of wood used to make the tools. With persistence, you should be able to produce a sustainable fire ready for cooking.

COOKING FIRES

Cooking your food in a survival situation has many advantages, and one main disadvantage. The disadvantage is that cooking food over heat, particularly boiling, kills many of the vitamins and nutrients. However, improvised cooking techniques are an inescapable part of surviving in the wild. Cooking makes many unpalatable survival foods taste better, delicious even, and also makes tough, fibrous foods more digestible. Most importantly, cooking kills bacteria, germs and parasites, which outweighs any concerns about the nutritional value.

The type of fire you make can help or hinder your attempts at survival cooking. There are basically five types of fire, some of them more sophisticated than others: the Yukon stove, the trench fire, the mud oven, the steam pit and the hobo stove.

Yukon stove

The Yukon stove takes time to build, but once it is up, it is excellent for heat and for cooking.

Begin by digging a circular hole in the ground about 9in (24cm) in diameter and about 1ft (30cm) deep. At one point on the circumference of this hole, dig a channel leading down into the hole. The fire's superstructure is built upon this hole. Building around the edge of the hole, stack up rocks to form a funnel shape – larger stones will be needed to bridge the gap created by the channel. This funnel should narrow towards the middle and flare out slightly at the top. As you build, pack any spaces between the

Fire safety

While fire is an essential tool for your survival, it can also be very dangerous. Obey the following safety practices when making and maintaining any fire:

● Remove any explosive materials to a safe distance from the fire. These materials include ammunition, stove fuel, matches, flares and batteries.

● Clear the fire area of any vegetation that may catch fire.

● Do not put porous or wet rocks on the fire. When heated, these rocks can explode like bombs, projecting dangerous fragments of rock at high speeds.

● Do not construct sleeping platforms too close to a fire.

● Avoid littering the fire area with any survival equipment.

● Do not allow a fire to blaze while you are sleeping. Place two or three big logs on the fire to keep it smouldering until dawn.

● When leaving a fire for good, extinguish it thoroughly, scatter the ashes to cool and then bury them in the ground.

Preparing a tepee fire

The simplest of all fires to build is a tepee fire. As its name suggests, the tepee fire starts with a tepee-like structure of kindling built up with an opening around the base for tinder to be inserted. The tinder is lit just outside the tepee, and is then pushed into the structure through the opening. The high, pointed tepee structure allows air to be conducted efficiently and provides numerous paths for the fire to work its way up. Once the kindling has fully taken, it can be collapsed and larger pieces of fuel placed on the fire.

Constructing a Yukon Stove

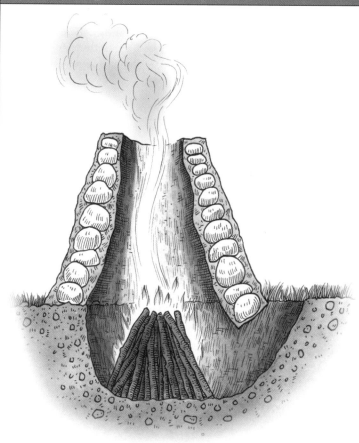

The Yukon Stove produces considerable heat, indeed a similar design of fire was used by older societies in the practice of iron smelting. Food is cooked over the chimney or is inserted into the heart of the oven via the fuel channel. This latter technique of cooking is only used if the fire inside has died down to coals, as a blazing Yukon fire will reduce foodstuffs to cinders.

placed over the vent at the top for cooking. The heat of the fire is controlled by restricting the amount of air accessible to the fire through the top of the funnel. This type of fire is so efficient – it burns long and intensely – that much of the ash from the burning wood is consumed. So the fire requires little cleaning out.

Trench fire

As its name suggests, the trench fire is quite simply a fire constructed in the bottom of a trench or ditch. This trench should be rectangular in shape and dug about 12in (30cm) wide, 36in (90cm) long and 18in (45cm) deep. The bottom of the trench is lined with a layer of rocks to radiate heat and protect the fire from the damp earth. A fire is made upon these rocks. Food can then be roasted or grilled on the mouth of the trench.

Mud oven

The mud oven is a more advanced cooking fire that requires a large fireproof pot or tin, not something that everyone will possess on a survival adventure. However, if one is available, this oven is excellent for cooking. Dig a narrow trench, narrower than the width of the pot, and place the pot on its side alongside the trench. Ensure that there is a gap underneath the pot for making a fire. Now take a long, thick stick and jam it upright in the ground at the base of the pot. Start covering

rocks with clay or earth to give an airtight seal and greater stability.

When this structure is built, start the fire in the channel and then push it into the hole beneath the funnel and feed with sticks dropped in through the top. This oven will produce considerable heat, and food can be

Cooking with a trench fire

A trench fire has a useful cooking application. While the main fire can blaze at one end of the trench and provide heat, embers can be scraped to the other end of the trench and used to cook on. When the trench is initially dug, leave it for about half and hour to see if it fills up with underground water – find another site if it does.

the pot with a substantial covering of earth or wet clay – leaving the lid free – eventually creating a mud dome around the entire pot. The long stick should protrude from the top of the dome. Now remove the stick. The resulting hole acts as a chimney for the fire while the stick can be put to use securing the lid during cooking. With a fire built under the pot, the mud oven is great for roasting and baking.

Hobo stove
The Hobo stove is a cheap and cheerful oven that requires a large metal drum (ideally something like a 5-gallon/23-litre metal drum). Punch a series of holes in the drum

Preparing a mud oven

A mud oven is one of the more advanced cooking systems, but is surprisingly quick to build. The heat generated inside the oven is high during cooking, and the oven is ideal for roasting, baking and even making bread. 4400-year-old mud oven constructions have recently been discovered in the Syrian deserts.

around the bottom circumference, and tear an opening panel immediately above to allow you to make a fire in the interior of the drum. Punch two more holes in the side of the drum just below the top to let out smoke. With a fire burning inside the drum, the top plate becomes hot enough to act as a griddle for frying, and the overall heat pro-duced by the drum gives out general warmth to the surroundings.

With this range of fires at your disposal, you should be able to tackle with confidence any sort of survival cookery. Of course, it is unlikely that you will have the materials to make all of these fires, and the type of fire

Building a steam pit

Preparing a steam pit is quite involved but the resulting 'oven' cooks food gently and with minimal loss of nutrients, so it is well worth the effort. First, you should make a stick platform over a trench and make a fire on it. Then, place a layer of rocks on the platform and leave the rocks to heat up (A). Eventually, the platform burns away and the hot rocks drop into the bottom of the trench. Next, clear away the glowing embers (using a brush of green twigs), push a long stick into the cen-

tre of the pit, and then cover with a thick layer of green grass. Place the meat, wrapped tightly in a binding of leaves, in the centre of this oven (B). Cover the meat package with another layer of grass (C) and then spread a good layer of earth over the entire pit, right up to the edges. Remove the now protruding stick and pour a small quantity of water into the hole (D). This runs down onto the rocks and creates steam. Finally, completely seal the pit with earth and allow the food to cook in the subterranean steam. Leave for about an hour to cook before removing from the pit and eating.

you make may well be determined by your environment and the materials to hand.

COOKING METHODS

Cooking methods will often be dictated by factors such as the type of fuel available, whether you have sufficient supplies of water for boiling, and the prevailing weather conditions. There are eight basic types of survival cookery: boiling, steaming, roasting, grilling, baking, frying, cooking on rocks, and cooking in clay.

Boiling

Boiling is one of the most accessible and fail-safe methods as long as you have enough fresh water to spare and an appropriate container. First, make a pot rod. This simply consists of a forked branch planted in the ground, with a long branch resting on the fork, with one end securely weighted to the ground with rocks. The other end of the branch hangs over the fire. You can suspend a metal container from this end. The pot rod provides a secure structure for the boiling can.

If no metal can is available, you can improvise a boiling vessel using birch bark. Cut out a large rectangular section of bark and then roll it into a cone-shape. Stitch or tie this into place around the top and down the seam. This is not the most durable container, but you will still be able to use it as a temporary vessel for boiling. Be careful, however, that the water does not dry out or the container will ignite. When boiling vegetables, cook for as long as is necessary to make them soft, extending the cooking time by up to 30 minutes in the case of tough and stringy roots or if you feel the vegetables are in questionable condition. Remember to save the fluid for drinking afterwards because it will contain valuable nutrients, unless you are boiling the foodstuffs to remove poisons. Meat should be cut into cubes about 1in (2.5cm) square and boiled for between 20 minutes and one hour. Fish will take only

around 10 minutes. Feel free to combine many different foods in one boiling pot to make a nourishing stew.

Steaming

Steaming, a variation on boiling, retains more of the food's nutrients because they cannot

Using a Hobo stove

Hobo stoves burn extremely hot because the holes at the top and bottom of the can create a powerful through-draft which fuels the fire. Partially obstructing the inlet hole or turning it away from the wind can help to control the temperature. Cooking can be done on the top of the can or by placing pans on the top in the manner of a stove.

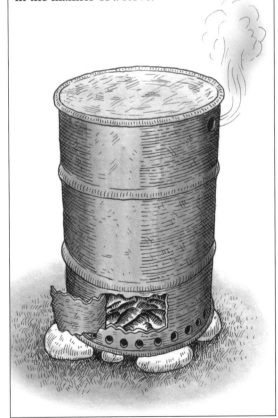

seep away into the water. To make a steamer, punch several holes in a can and suspend it in the larger boiling vessel. Make sure that this inner can does not touch the boiling water. Place the vegetables in the steamer and then put a lid over the top of both vessels, making it as tight as possible without running the risk of pressure building up to explosion point. Steaming is best reserved for cooking vegetables.

Roasting

The pot rod used for boiling can also be used for roasting – simply turn the exposed end of the stick into a spit. A better method of presenting meat to the fire, however, is to build a rotatable spit. Put two forked branches into the ground, one on each side of the fire. Spit and centre the meat on a long stick and then suspend the stick across the fire on the forked branches. When roasting meat, it is important to catch the nutritionally valuable fat that drips from the meat during cooking. To do this, offset the meat a little from the fire and place a drip tray beneath it.

Roasting meat should be done with caution, as the intense heat of the fire can mean that the outside looks cooked while the inside remains raw and unsafe to eat. To test any red or white meat, stab a knife or skewer into its centre and remove it. If red juices bubble out of the cut, then the meat is still bloody inside, and needs more cooking. Another check is to press the knife carefully against your skin after you have withdrawn it. If the blade is very hot, it means that the food is cooking inside; if it is cool, the meat is still not safe to eat.

Vegetables can also be roasted successfully, and they have the advantage of not losing as many nutrients as when boiled. For very resilient vegetables such as roots, you may need to parboil the vegetables before roasting.

Grilling

Grilling (also known as broiling) is, in most senses, the same as roasting, except that the foodstuffs are suspended over the fire by a mesh instead of a spit. This mesh can be a professional camping grill, or it can be improvised using very green twigs. Grilling, however, does not provide the opportunity to catch the dripping animal fats, so only use this method when you are confident of your food supplies.

Where to position your fire

If a fire is to be safe and effective, it must be positioned correctly.

- Find somewhere sheltered. A large rock behind the fire can be useful because it will reflect heat onto your back if you sit between the rock and the fire.
- Clear a circle of earth about 6.5ft (2m) in diameter right down to the bare earth. Position your fire in the centre of this circle.
- Set your fire on a platform of rocks or green branches if the ground is wet or snow-covered.
- Don't build fires at the base of trees or anything else that may catch fire.
- Build your fire in a location close to good sources of fuel so that you don't have to keep travelling too far to collect fuel for the fire.
- Make sure that your fire is not positioned under deadwood boughs extending from nearby trees. These may fall down on you as they dry out.

Baking in mud

Delicate meats such as fish can be cooked using the mud baking technique. The fish is first wrapped in green leaves to form a tight parcel (A) and (B). This parcel is then covered in a thick layer of mud or clay (C) and a fire is made over the top of it (D). As the clay heats up the water content of the leaves inside is released, keeping the fish moist during the baking process. At the end of cooking the mud will have hardened and can simply be cracked off.

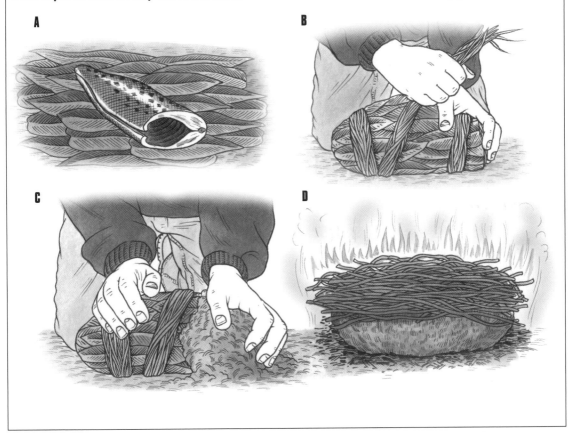

A

B

C

D

Baking

Baking foods generally requires the construction of a mud oven. As you are unlikely to be rustling up cakes and bread in a survival situation, baking is normally used to cook meat. The primary advantage of baking is that old, gristly or tough meat is tenderized by the longer, slower process of cooking. Also, all fats that drip from the meat are caught in the oven (though it is best to set the meat in a tray for cooking). These fats should be used to baste the meat during cooking, but if you have fat to spare, baste some root vegetables and put them in the oven as well. Oven baking allows you to cook many different foods at once.

Frying

Frying tends to get a bad press in the 'civilized' world, mainly because it's associated with a marked increase in heart disease and some forms of cancer. In a survival situation, however, frying has positive benefits. It infuses food with the energy-rich fat needed for sustenance during intense physical challenges. Frying simply requires fat and a metal sheet or container on which to fry. If you only have a sheet, try to bend the edges to form a lip.

Cooking on rocks

Cooking on hot rocks is essentially the survival equivalent of barbecuing. Make campfires on a bed of rocks, and then, when the flames have died down and the wood has burnt away, the rocks will remain hot enough to cook on. Brush away any embers from the rocks with a handful of green twigs and place the meat or vegetables straight

Cooking on hot rocks

Cooking on hot rocks involves starting a fire on a platform of rocks (A and B), brushing away the embers after the fire has died down (C) and then placing the food directly onto the hot rocks (D). The rocks must be selected with caution. Avoid porous rocks, or rocks which have been submerged in water. If a rock contains water the fluid will boil upon heating and could result in the stone exploding with considerable force.

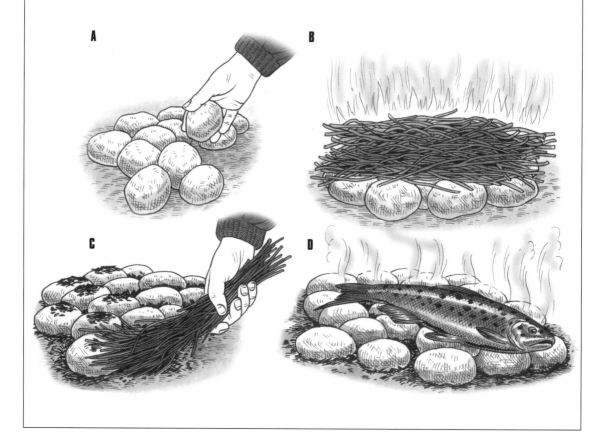

onto the stones, turning frequently. The rocks will be cooler on the outside of the fire than in the centre, so if meat needs to be cooked for a long time, start on the outside rocks and move slowly towards the centre to take advantage of all available heat.

An even slower method of cooking – good for larger pieces of meat or tough vegetables – is to build the rocks into an oven structure. Place a thick layer of rocks in a pit and light a fire over them. As usual, once the fire has died down, brush the embers away to expose the rocks and place your food on top. Then cover over the pit with branches and a thick layer of earth and leaves. With the heat of the rocks trapped inside the pit, the food is cooked slowly in the manner of a pressure cooker over 1.5–2 hours.

Cooking in clay

The final survival cooking method is cooking in clay or mud. This technique is only really suitable for meats. Wrap a piece of meat or fish in a solid pack of clay or, alternatively, a wrap of mud covered over with green leaves and grass. Place these parcels directly onto the embers of a fire, and then build a further fire over the top of them. The mud and clay act as insulators and stop the meat burning while drawing in enough heat to cook the contents. Clay cooking has another virtue: when the clay is removed after cooking, it will pull off fish scales, birds' feathers and even hedgehog spines, saving you some time on food preparation. For this reason, avoid cooking vegetables by this method, as you will loose the wholesome vegetable skin.

PRESERVING FOOD

Food preservation techniques provide you with supplies to last some time, and so reduce the amount of time you need to spend foraging and hunting. Preservation also combats the germs and micro-organisms that start to flourish the moment food

is caught or gathered. As a general preservation measure, try to keep all foods as cool as possible, in airtight containers and out of direct sunlight. Of course that won't be possible in every survival situation, so drying, smoking and salting are the best ways of keeping food edible.

Drying

Drying works by reducing or removing the water content of foods to below 5 per cent of mass, which makes it difficult for moulds to form. Also, insects lose some of their interest in the food. Drying is best used on non-fatty meats such as fish and poultry and fungi; fatty meats can be dried but you will have to trim off as much fat as possible for the method to be effective.

Foods can be dried in the wind and sun, but both must be strong and there must be no moisture in the air. The aim is to let the food dry out before it goes off, so start the drying process immediately – drying can take several days to complete. Place vegetables on warm rocks in the sun, and hang meats over an improvised wooden frame (or simply over tree branches) with as much of the flesh exposed to the air as possible. With all meats, trim them into small lean fillets or chunks before drying, and rub salt into fatty sections to assist the withdrawal of moisture. If there is no sunlight, place the food above an open fire, though not close enough to cook it. Because of their protective shells, nuts can be set directly on the embers of a fire. Drying by fire is a fine art, and takes some practice to get it right.

Drying berries constitutes a special case. Many berries have watertight skins which prevents the evaporation of their water content. In the case of non-segmented berries such as blueberries and juneberries, slice each berry open to expose the inner flesh. Then place the opened berry on the drying surface with the inner flesh exposed to the air. Do not lay this flesh against the drying surface as it will glue itself there as it dries out. For segmented fruits such as raspberries and blackberries this method will not work, as each segment is watertight. Instead puree these fruit in a container and then spread the puree over a clean, detachable surface (such as a sheet of non-porous material) to dry.

Food is considered 'dried out' when it is dry to the touch and is brittle or crumbly under pressure. In this state it can be stored as it is or, in the case of fruit and vegetables, ground up into a powder. The powder can be used as a nutritional thickening agent to soups and stews. When reconstituting a dried food, either soak in water for several hours or boil for about 30–60 minutes.

Smoking

Smoking is possibly the most effective way of drying food. Smoke, like air drying, dehydrates but also leaves a waxy coating on the surface of the food that prevents moisture being absorbed.

Smoking food should be done using a construction known as a smoke tepee. To build this, first make a tepee-like structure using three long, straight branches tied at their intersection. About halfway up the inside of this structure, make a lattice platform out of small, green branches and tie it securely to the supporting struts. Then, start a fire in the base of the tepee. Wait for the fire to reduce to a smoulder before throwing on large piles of green leaves (not grass, conifer needles or holly). These will start to smoulder and produce a heavy smoke. Now place strips of meat or fish onto the smoking platform before covering the entire tepee over with a cloth or branches and pieces of turf (leave a small air gap for the fire). Once enclosed, leave the food to smoke for around 18 hours to ensure it is fully dehydrated.

Salting

Salting works because of salt's ability to absorb moisture when applied to food. Simply smearing a piece of fish or meat with salt will retard its decay slightly. It is far more effective, however, to store the food between layers of salt (wash the salt off before use). Alternatively, boil meat or vegetables in brine (a salt solution). While the boiling kills any germs on the food, the salt in the water acts as a preservative once the food is taken out.

Drying, smoking and salting are not the only means of preserving food. Fish can be soaked in lime or lemon juice after boiling, and vegetables can be preserved by boiling

Preparing an oil and water fire

An oil and water fire is one of the hottest fires you can make. Take two tins cans and make a small hole in the bottom of each. Plug these holes with twigs and fill one can with water and the other with oil. Hang the two cans from a branch with the puncture holes suspended over a piece of guttering which leads down to a metal plate set on four stones, with a fire underneath to heat the plate. Now loosen the pegs in the cans to allow the water and oil to drip into the trough (three parts water to one oil) and run onto the plate. When the water and oil mix on the plate, they will ignite, producing a very hot flame. Another metal plate placed on the rocks over this flame makes an excellent surface for frying.

Make your own drying frame

A drying frame works by maximizing the surface area of food exposed to drying elements such as wind, smoke and sun. It should be constructed from hardwoods which exude little sap or flavour to the food. If built on a large enough scale a fire can be started in the centre of the frame for smoking food. A large frame can usefully double as a shelter when covered with a waterproof sheet.

with pickling spices. Another excellent technique of preserving fish is to make a pemmican. A pemmican is made from a combination of flaked, dried fish mixed with an equal amount of animal fat into a ball. Sealed in a bag, the pemmican will provide you with a nutritious meal (it contains every vitamin and mineral except vitamin C) that can remain edible, in colder climates, for over a year.

CHAPTER SEVEN

Surviving in the desert

Desert survival is hazardous in the extreme, as both food and water are usually in short supply. The survivor must understand the terrain to find adequate water, and be prepared to eat some unpalatable foods to stay alive.

Deserts occupy over 20 per cent of the earth's surface. The Sahara Desert alone is 3,000,000 square miles (7,700,000 square kilometres) in area, and the Gobi Desert over 400,000 square miles (1,040,000 square kilometres). By definition, a desert is a place that receives less than 10in (25cm) of rain each year. This chronic lack of water is usually, but not always, combined with extremely high temperatures. For example, in 1992 the midday heat in El Azizia, Libya, rose to a blistering 136°F (58°C), one of the highest temperatures ever recorded on earth. More common daytime temperatures in the equatorial deserts of Africa, Australia, America and the Middle East usually reach over 45°C (113°F) during the summer period. By night, the situation is reversed. Cloudless skies produce a night chill that,

particularly in the winter months, can lower temperatures to -10°C (14°F).

There are many obstacles to survival in desert regions apart from the extreme heat. Torrential desert rains produce flash-floods and mudslides. Dust storms reduce visibility to a matter of inches and coat the body with a choking dust. Mirages, created by the distortion of light passing through heat rising from the desert floor, create illusions of hills, trees and animals. Together, the features of any desert landscape make it an inhospitable place for survival. Whatever the conditions, the first priority in a desert is always to find water within the first few hours.

FINDING WATER IN THE DESERT

Dehydration and heat exhaustion are the greatest threats in the desert. The very hot and dry climate accelerates sweat evaporation and so the body loses more of its stored fluids. A person exerting himself in a desert climate will lose between 17 and 21 pints (10–12 litres) of body fluid each day. When dehydration occurs, the body releases enzymes that slow the rate of water loss and increase the sensation of thirst. Without more fluids the body will experience severe dehydration, usually within 24 hours.

To date, the record for survival without water in the desert goes to Pablo Valencia, a Mexican who became lost in the Tinajas Atlas desert area of Arizona in 1905. Even at night, temperatures never dropped below 85°F (29°C). When he was found close to death after seven days and nights without food or water, his eyelids and lips had been burnt off by the sun, his entire body was blackened, he was deaf and practically blind, and he could not speak or swallow. Fortunately, he was found by colleagues from a nearby camp. He had lost over 18lb (8kg) in body fluids. They began the rehydration process immediately, and in three days all his senses had returned and he made a full recovery.

Valencia's desert survival story is, however, exceptional. It is common for people lost in the desert to be dead by the end of the first day. Delirium sets in after about 10 per cent water loss, and the survivor loses the ability to track down water sources. The survivor must conserve and protect existing water supplies, inside and outside the body.

Water sources in the desert

This desert landscape offers three main sources of water. The pool in the middle provides open water, though this could be stagnant and poisonous. The well on the left would be more profitable, though as it has been left uncovered it may have dried out. The dry river bed will probably have underground water beneath it, suggested by the healthy palm trees near it.

This means not using water unnecessarily and rationing out remaining water supplies. Only use water for drinking, medical treatments or preparing food.

Daily water needs

Water weighs about 8.3lb (3.8kg) per gallon, so unless you are travelling in a vehicle, it is unlikely that you will be carrying very large amounts. The US military estimates that a working soldier needs about 4 gallons (15 litres) of drinking water each day to stave off dehydration. In a survival situation all physical activity is kept to an absolute limit, and 4 gallons (15 litres) of water would be luxury. However, walking at night requires about 1 gallon (3.8 litres) for every 20 miles (32km) covered, and 2 gallons (7.6 litres) for the same distance covered during the day. When resting, 2 gallons (7.6 litres) should last about three to five days. Ration water evenly over the period, though half a pint (0.2 litre) a day should be your absolute minimum. For the first day without water, military survival experts recommend not drinking at all because your body has a store that will see you through 24 hours. This is basically good advice, but it might need to be adjusted to take account of personal circumstances. If water intake has been low prior to the emergency, or if you

have to work hard under the desert sun, water depletion may reach critical levels, even on the first day. If you feel in any way delirious, start to drink. Also, start collecting additional water immediately to build up reserve supplies.

Conserving body fluids is vital in the desert. The most important point to remember is not to remove any clothing in an attempt to cool down. Clothing traps perspiration, and the wet clothing acts as a cooling layer against the skin. Removing clothes simply allows the perspiration to evaporate, increasing your need for water. Keep shirtsleeves rolled down, wear a neck scarf and hat, and keep clothing loose to trap some cooling air between it and your skin. Walk only at night when the temperature is cooler. Always remember that winds, though they might feel cool, actually increase the rate of evaporation from the skin.

Rains and rivers

Finding desert water requires knowledge of the local geology and flora. The tracks and trails of nomadic herdsmen are useful, as they will lead to watering holes at regular intervals. However, these intervals may vary from every 19 miles (30km) to every 160 miles (100km), and on foot you might not cover 10 miles (16km) in a day.

Reducing the feeling of thirst

Thirst is a near-permanent sensation in arid regions. However, there are measures to take that can reduce its discomfort. Keep your mouth closed as much as possible. If you breathe through the mouth, the influx of hot air will constantly dry out any

moisture on your tongue and palate. Sucking small stones or even buttons can help produce more saliva, though do not do this while on the move because there's a danger you might swallow the object. If you have salt with you, only consume it when you take a

drink of water. Salt taken at other times will only increase thirst. Do not smoke or drink alcohol. Smoke dehydrates flesh on contact and will suck moisture out of your mouth, while alcohol only causes frequent urination and, therefore, further water loss.

Extracting water from a dry river bed

An apparently dried-up river bed may still contain underground water. The best part of the river bed to explore is the outside of a bend. Kalahari bushmen extract water from these locations by inserting a long hollow reed down into the soil and sucking on it. After about 10 minutes of sucking, water usually starts to flow up the reed.

Surface water does exist in desert areas but mainly in the period immediately after rain. Rains can occur once a year in the winter or sporadically throughout the year, depending on the desert. In one or two desert locations, you will find large, permanent rivers that never dry out because of their size, for example, the Nile, the Colorado or the Kuiseb in the Namib Desert of southwest Africa. Water taken from any of these rivers must be thoroughly purified, as they are all major channels for disease, parasites and bacteria.

Plants as indicators

Local plant and animal life can also help you to find smaller patches of open water. The tracks of grazing animals may converge towards a watering hole. Birds such as parrots, pigeons, the Asian sand grouse, crested larks and zebra birds visit watering holes at least once a day.

Plants also grow around any water source, whether it's above or below ground. Cattails, cottonwoods, palms, greasewoods, willows, elderberry, rushes and salt grass are useful indicators of underground water. They grow only where water is accessible beneath the surface. A palm tree suggests that water is only 3ft (1m) below, while salt grass draws on water 6.5ft (2m) underground. The water that feeds cottonwood is up to 12ft (4m) below and will take some energetic digging to reach. Observe the behaviour of desert animals for further indications of underground water. Flies may be seen swarming over a patch of ground, or mammals might scratch at the earth in the attempt to reach underground water.

Desert terrain

The desert terrain itself provides more important clues about where to look for water. Limestone cliffs or rocky outcrops are well worth investigating because limestone is one of the most easily dissolved rocks. Limestone systems, therefore, are often littered with underground water-storage caverns and passages. Look to see if there are any springs or seepages from the face of the rock, and explore any caverns, if it is safe to do so. Check that the caverns are free from dangerous wild animals before exploring too deeply inside, as desert creatures use caves for shelter from the daytime heat. Lava rock or sandstone areas may also contain water, as both types of stone are porous. Explore places where canyons or valleys cut through sections of the rock, and check the rock walls for seepages.

Apart from specific rock formations, any sheltered corner of the desert might yield some water, so be prepared to travel widely. Dry riverbeds look particularly unpromising, but underground water often soaks into the soil and remains there for long periods. The best place to investigate is at the outside edge of a bend in the river. Simply dig down to a depth of several feet with a spade or improvised tool until the hole becomes damp. Stop digging at this point and the hole should begin to fill with water. Have a container at the ready to catch it.

Plant life

Desert peoples also extract water from certain plants. During the night and early morning, dew often collects on desert grasses. Collect this by rubbing over the grass with a rag, then wringing out the water into a container. Water can also be found in plants themselves. Aborigines in the Australian outback frequently rely on the roots of the desert oak, water tree and bloodwood for water. Dig up the roots and cut them into lengths about 24–36in (60–91cm) long. Then, strip off the bark and suck the root to extract its water.

Of all water-storing plants in the desert, cacti hold the most significant quantities of usable fluid. Not all species of cacti contain water, and some actually pollute their water content with a poisonous sap. The barrel cactus, however, is one of the safest for drinking water, and also one of the most easily recognized cacti. It grows in the southern US and in some parts of South America, grows up to 4ft (1.2m) and has a distinctive barrel shape. To get at the pulpy interior, cut off the top of the cactus – a strenuous and exhausting job. Chopping out and crushing this pulp should produce about 2 pints (1 litre) of a watery, milky fluid that is fit for drinking. Prickly pears also contain useable amounts of water in their fruit and main segments, while carrion flowers – so called because of the stench of rotting meat exuded by the star-shape flowers – hold water in their stems. Chop and crush as with the barrel cactus.

Other water-bearing plants include vines and palm trees (see chapter nine). Along with underground sources, these plants should provide you with enough water for survival purposes. In places where even

Extracting water from a cactus

Extracting water from a barrel cactus involves slicing off the top of the cactus (A) and mashing the interior flesh into a pulp (B). Once this is done the pulp can be either squeezed to extract the water or a hollow reed is inserted into the pulp to drink directly from the cactus (C).

underground water and plants are scarce, you may have to rely on tools such as the solar still. Unless, however, you have several stills, they will rarely provide enough water for all your needs.

Animals

One more water source remains – animals. When you have killed an animal for food, sucking on its eyes – as horrific as it sounds – will give you a small shot of water. Its blood will also provide you with fluid and nutrients. A more substantial drink can be taken from desert frogs in north-western Australia. These frogs survive in arid conditions by storing water in their bodies and then protecting themselves from the heat by creating an underground burrow in clay soils. If these frogs are found and dug up, they can be squeezed out like a sponge to provide a drink.

DESERT HUNTING AND ANIMAL FOODS

The best time for hunting in the desert is in the early morning or the early evening. At these times, just prior to, and just after, the intense heat of the day, many animals are at their most active and clearly visible. Grazing animals will find waterholes, lizards will be hunting for insects, and birds are more likely to take to the wing. Also, by hunting at these times, you avoid depleting your body's water and energy through exposure to daytime temperatures.

There are some advantages, however, to braving the daytime heat for a short time. Because most animals take shelter in the daytime, they are more easily tracked. Reptiles gravitate to the shade of rocks or caves – so turn over rocks and logs with a stick and be prepared to strike quickly if you find anything. Mammals and birds gather beneath the shade of the branches of isolated trees. However, do not spend long hunting under the daytime sun. Unless you find and kill prey quickly, the major disadvantage of water loss will outweigh the benefits of a successful kill.

Night hunting

Hunting after dark is also a viable option, as the cloudless skies of most deserts result in brilliant clear nights with good visibility, especially if the moon is full. The downside

Safe hunting in the desert

When hunting in arid regions, follow these principles of movement to ensure your safety:

- Have a clear idea of where you are going and how to get back. In sandy regions, remember that landmarks may be obscured by drifting sand hours after you first see them, which can confuse your sense of

direction. Follow roads, paths, trails and coast-lines.
- Deep sand or high sand dunes are exhausting to walk over and will increase your rate of water loss. Select flatter, harder terrain for hunting if possible.
- Follow shelter as much as possible. Walk on the lee-ward side of hills and

beneath rocky overhangs.
- If you see rainclouds approaching, move to high ground to avoid the danger of flash-floods.
- In a sandstorm, lie down on your side with your back to the wind. Sand will build up against your back but will not bury you. Cover your face with a cloth to protect your eyes and nose.

is that human beings have poor night senses compared with most other animals. The still night air of the desert also transmits sound very effectively over long distances, and cautious animals are quick to pick up on the least suspicious noise. Unless the hunter is very accomplished, at night an animal will usually sense his human presence long before he can close his hunting distance.

A desert may appear flat, but a closer look will usually reveal undulations and low and high ground. When hunting, stay in depressions when travelling to reduce your silhouette. If moving through savannah, attach natural grasses to your head and shoulders as camouflage. Desert peoples tend to hunt using projectile weapons, as it is more difficult to use traps in dry flatlands with little vegetation. Strike while animals are drinking or resting. If you are following a herd or group, go for straggling animals, though be careful that they are not diseased, as they will be inedible. Handle a carcass quickly once you have made your kill. In areas of Africa, big cats and scavenging birds and dogs will appear within minutes of a kill to see what they can get for themselves. If possible, drag the body up a tree, or at least perform some very quick butchery and take with you whatever meat you can carry.

Daytime hunting

During the hot daytime hours, hunters will experience problems with their vision. Refraction caused by heat rising from the desert floor bends the light between target and viewer. During the day, this mainly occurs when there are clear skies, very flat terrain and a wind speed of less than 10mph (16km/h). At night the wind speed needs to be less than 5mph (8km/h). The effect is that, in the day, the target looks lower than it actually is, while at night the opposite happens. Note that significant refraction is more likely at ranges in excess of 1524ft (500m), so long-range rifle shots are the most affected. However, the optical displacement of the target may lead you into stalking the animal along the wrong route. Such problems are made worse by the fact that, in the desert, objects seem closer than they really are. What you think is only a few hundred feet/metres away could be well over a mile distant. Again, the moral is that it is generally inadvisable to hunt in the heat of the day.

Edible animals

Despite its apparent barrenness, a desert environment can still yield a surprising number of edible animals. Most desirable of all are the large mammals such as wildebeest, antelope of various kinds, big cats, zebras

Categories of termite

Termites contain 35.2 per cent fat and 45.6 per cent protein, and so are an excellent survival food. Apart from the large king and queen termites, which can grow up to 4.7in (12cm) long, there are three basic forms of termite; a winged termite capable of reproduction (known as a 'sexual'), a wingless termite which cannot reproduce ('non-sexual'), and a small worker termite.

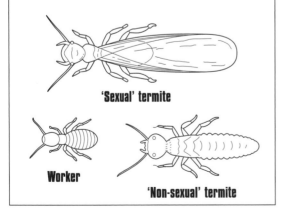

'Sexual' termite

Worker

'Non-sexual' termite

Making a water trap for termites

A smooth-sided pot is inserted up to the rim in the ground with water in the bottom. A board or similar covering is placed over the pot propped up on four rocks to create a gap between the board and the earth. The insects crawl beneath the board in search of shelter and moisture and then drop into the pot and are trapped.

and giraffes. These animals are only to be found in tropical or subtropical grasslands or semi-desert regions. However, in Africa, some species of antelope, including the gazelle and the scimitar-horned oryx, survive solely on the moisture extracted from desert plants, and are therefore to be found in even the most arid of regions. Both are wary creatures that can move at great speed, and the combined senses of the herd make them hard to track at close range. Horned antelope are also equipped to defend themselves with considerable aggression and should not be tackled at close range. Do not, as a rule, tackle a large mammal without a gun or a powerful projectile weapon.

Hunting dogs proliferate in desert areas. Australia has its dingoes, the US its coyotes, and Africa its hyenas and jackals. Hunting dogs are most active at night. As much of their fluid intake is derived from animal blood, look out for any animal carcasses to use as bait. Firearms are best for killing hunting dogs because the loud shots scare away other dogs. If you don't have a gun, then try to spear one creature and scare the others away with a flaming torch. Hunting dogs encountered in very large packs are best left alone.

Smoking out a rabbit

Smoke directed into a rabbit's hole will flush the creature out, and it can be clubbed with a large stick as it emerges from the hole (shown below). Alternatively, a snare can be placed at the mouth of the hole, which has the advantage of relieving the hunter from his vigilant watch. The snare is best applied to rabbit holes set in dense foliage where the snare wire will be less conspicuous and more easily concealed.

In Australia, kangaroos and wallabies are another food option. Stalk them to close range and kill with a throwing stick or bola (if not a gun) aimed at the head. Red kangaroos are the most prolific, and are generally regarded as a nuisance by the locals. They can grow to more than 4ft (1.1m) tall and will put up a vigorous defence if threatened. The 'boxing' kangaroo is not a myth – they can deliver powerful, lacerating blows with their forelegs, while a double-legged kick from the back legs can be fatal to a human.

Birds

Birds-of-prey and carrion birds are a much better food option in the desert. They make excellent prey because they are easy to bait and locate. Any animal carcass in the desert will attract them in large numbers, and all it takes to catch them are chunks of meat attached to hooked pins tied to a line. However, as using meat may not be an option, and as the birds usually gather in large numbers, it is easily possible to make a kill just by throwing a large sharp stick at them.

Mammals and reptiles

The many varieties of small ground-dwelling mammals and reptiles are a good source of desert food. Mice, rats and rabbits are usually plentiful, as are many other rodents such as the desert jerboas and gerbils of the Sahara, the prairie dogs of the deserts of north-west Mexico, and the desert hamsters of east Asia. Most of these animals are burrowing creatures. Digging them up can be difficult because some burrows are labyrinthine and feature concealed escape routes. Trapping is the best option if the burrow entrances are surrounded by vegetation. Otherwise, try keeping a vigil outside a burrow in the early evening, and strike the creature with a stick as it warily emerges. With some rodents and rabbits, lamping also works fairly well in remote desert regions, as most of the indigenous animals are unaccustomed to artificial light.

The desert has an abundant supply of reptiles suitable to eat. Snakes and lizards are found sheltering beneath rocks and stones during the daytime heat. With snakes, however, exercise caution. The desert regions are home to some of the world's most poisonous varieties, including rattlesnakes, coral snakes (in the Americas), puff adders and cobras (Africa), and death adders and tiger snakes (Australia). In addition, the deserts have two very dangerous types of large lizard. One, the gila monster, which inhabits the desert areas of central America and Mexico, can grow up to 20in (50cm) long. It has a powerful poisonous bite that can result in fever, vomiting, fatigue and chronic systematic and localized infection. However, it is unlikely to bite without being provoked by being handled or stepped on. The larger beaded lizard, which inhabits the same regions and also has a poisonous bite, can grow up to 39in (100cm) in length.

Insects

Insects are the smallest creatures on the desert menu, but their sheer number means they are also the most important. Locusts tend to be plentiful in grasslands or agricultural areas and are best prepared like grasshoppers and crickets (remove the legs

Scorpion

There are two families of scorpions, the Buthids and the Scorpionids. The 520 species of Buthids are small in size, usually between 3 and 5in (8 and 12cm), but they contain the most poisonous scorpion types. The Scorpionids are larger creatures, growing up to 8in (21cm). Despite their ferocious appearance, most Scorpionid poison is relatively harmless to humans.

Locusts as food

Locusts are an important desert survival food. A dramatic method of catching them is to set fire to a strip of grassland. Locusts inhabiting the strip fly through the fire, singe their wings and drop to the ground for collection once the fire has burned out. It is vital to remove legs before eating, as they feature sharp bristles which can form a fatal intestinal blockage if ingested.

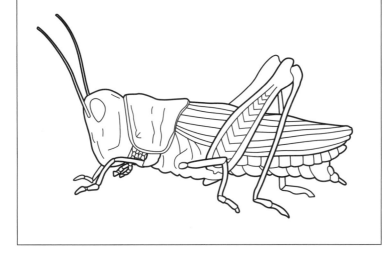

and wings before cooking). When they travel in swarms, sometimes numbering millions, they can be gathered in large quantities for a substantial meal. At ground level, various species of beetles proliferate. Most of these are edible once the wings and legs have been removed but, as always, follow the rule of avoiding brightly coloured creatures -- they may be poisonous.

DESERT PLANT FOODS

The desert climate means arid regions have less vegetation than temperate or tropical zones, but edible plants are still available there. Watering holes and rivers are the natural places to look for plant life, but even in the driest desert locations, edible plants can be found.

Edible desert plants

Name: Acacia (*Acacia*)
Description: Small to medium-sized tree with spiked branches and small leaflets. Ball-shaped white, pink or yellow flowers. Grows throughout Africa, Asia and Australia.
Eating notes: Leaves and shoots are edible when boiled; the seeds when roasted. Roots can be tapped for water.

Name: Baobab (*Adansonia*)
Description: Tree with massive swollen trunk (up to 30ft/9m in diameter); found throughout, Africa, the Middle East and Australia.
Eating notes: Large fruits are edible raw; young leaves edible when boiled. Roots also contain water.

Name: Carob (*Ceratonia siliqua*)
Description: Evergreen plant that grows to 50ft (15m) in locations across the Mediterranean, Africa, the Middle East and India. Red flowers with flat seed pods.
Eating notes: Seed pods contain edible pulp that requires no cooking. Seeds themselves can be ground up into powder and used to make porridge.

Name: Date palms (*Phoenix*)
Description: A tall palm tree. Long leaves with clusters of brown fruit. Located throughout North Africa, the Middle East and across to India.
Eating notes: Fruits are edible raw; young leaves edible after boiling. Trunk contains nutritious sugary sap.

Edible desert plants

Prickly Pears, Baobabs and Carob plants can be found throughout many of the world's deserts. If all are accessible, they will provide most vital vitamins and minerals, fibre to aid digestion, and the Prickly Pear and Baobab can be tapped for water from the stem and roots respectively.

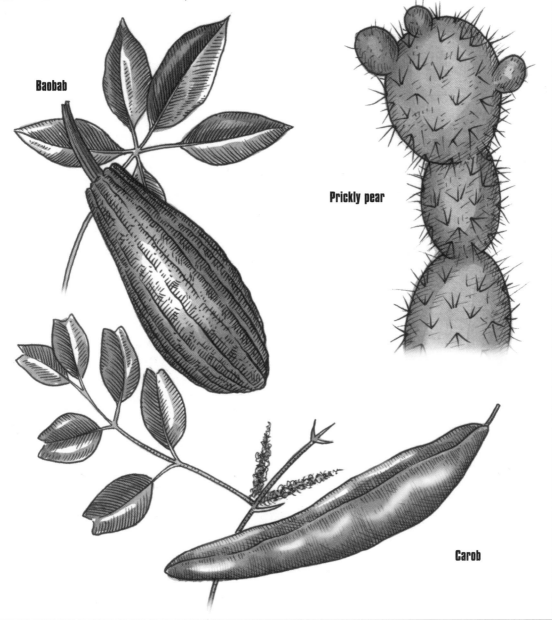

Baobab

Prickly pear

Carob

Name: Mescal (*Agave*)
Description: Long, straight flower stalk growing out of a cluster of tough, spiky leaves. Located in tropical and desert regions of Africa, Asia, the US and Mexico, and southern Europe.
Eating notes: If stalk is not flowering, it can be eaten after boiling.

Name: Prickly Pear (*Opuntia*)
Description: Large jointed pads for leaves, covered in sharp spines. Yellow or red flowers. Oval fruits.
Eating notes: Fruits are edible raw. Pads require peeling and boiling. Tap stems for water.

Name: Wild Gourds (*Cucurbitaceae*)
Description: Vine-like plant that creeps across ground and other surfaces in dense patterns. Produces large round fruits and yellow flowers.
Eating notes: Fruit, young leaves and seeds are edible when cooked (seeds require roasting). Chew stems and shoots to extract water.

Most desert regions will contain one or many of the above in significant numbers. Also, almost all desert grasses are edible. The best part to eat is the white, succulent root tip underground. Simply pull up a handful of grasses and snip the tips into a bowl. You can eat these either raw or cooked, though cooking usually makes them more palatable. Remember the rule of avoiding any plant that secretes a milky or coloured sap.

DESERT COOKING AND STORAGE

The desert's climate lends itself well to survival cooking and firelighting. In temperate and tropical zones, regular rainfall can make finding suitable dry tinder, kindling and fuel difficult. By contrast, the baking heat of the desert dries out branches, leaves and grasses until they are completely devoid of moisture.

Some arid regions, mainly those of Africa, are frequented by large herds of grazing animals such as wildebeest and antelope. The mass of dung left in their wake is excellent for fuel. The dung should be used in its dry state only and mixed with grass to control the rate of burn. Furthermore, it is best not to roast food directly over the dung as the smell imparted to the food can be unpalatable – use it to heat cooking surfaces such as rocks or metal plates.

A desert fire should be positioned in a sheltered site. Desert winds can be very strong, especially at night, and an exposed fire is likely to be scattered by the gusts. Be very diligent about clearing away any desert grasses from around your fire – they will be so dry that it will take little to set them alight. When starting a fire in the desert, use the climate to your advantage. While magnifying glasses are a hit-and-miss tool for starting fires in temperate climates, they are excellent in the desert for channelling the strong heat onto tinder. If you have a sheet of steel, leave it out in the sun until it becomes very hot, and then make a fire on top of it. It is possible that the temperature of the steel may be enough to ignite the tinder, but, if not, the heat it gives off will certainly make ignition that much easier. If you don't have a sheet of steel, use a hot, flat rock instead.

Steel and rocks have a further use in desert cooking. During World War II, soldiers in the North African campaign frequently used the steel and iron surfaces of tanks to cook on. Such was the temperature of the metal under the sun that no actual fire was needed. A standard vehicle shell is unlikely to get so hot, but it will transmit enough heat to dry out food very quickly.

Desert rocks make excellent improvised frying pans. Select a large, flat rock and support it on other rocks, leaving an air gap of about 12in (30cm). Make a fire under the rock and allow it to heat up. After about 20 minutes, the rock will be hot enough to act as a frying pan. Mountainous desert areas are frequently littered with rocks that have large depressions carved into them by erosion. These can be used as boiling vessels in the absence of normal pots.

Any food acquired in the desert should be eaten immediately if it cannot be preserved. The extreme heat encourages rapid decay and, in the case of animal foods, predators will soon pick up the scent of blood and make for your camp. Gut and prepare animal foods at the site of the kill – not back in your shelter. Many desert creatures can also smell water, so keep the lids on water bottles and all other water containers when they are not in use. Food should be kept out of direct sunlight and as cool as possible. To store meat for a couple of hours, wrap it tightly in a plastic bag and bury it underground beneath the shade of a rock. The combination of shade and ground moisture should keep the food reasonably cool.

In camp, protect food from ground-dwelling insects and rodents by hanging it from a tree branch. However, check the tree first to see if it is swarming with insects. For extra security, nail a box to the tree and use it as an improvised storage cupboard.

CHAPTER EIGHT

Surviving in Arctic climates

Polar climates generally offer very limited survival foods. The survivor in these climates must become adept at catching or sourcing a narrow range of foodstuffs which nonetheless provide all his nutritional needs.

The polar regions lie between 66° latitude and the north and south poles. In the north, the Arctic Circle consists of a frozen sea surrounded by a ring of landmasses that include parts of Greenland, Canada, Alaska, Norway, Sweden, Finland and the Russian Federation. The lands within the Arctic Circle suffer a permafrost (ie the earth is permanently frozen) but enjoy a surprisingly variable temperature – up to 65°F (18°C) in the summer, dipping to around –81°F (–56°C) in the winter However, within 70° latitude most of the Arctic Circle is a blank, frozen ocean. Because of the ice- and wind-chill here and in the glacial regions of Greenland, the temperatures never climb above freezing point.

The Antarctic consists of a base of continental rock capped by an ice sheet several miles thick. The climate is abnormally and consistently harsh. Even though the Antarctic receives plenty of sunshine in the winter months, the ice sheet reflects back about 80 per cent of the radiated warmth. Antarctica also has an average elevation of 7500ft (2300m) with very high wind speeds. Some areas have an average annual windspeed of 44mph (70km/h), but speeds of up to 110mph (177km/h) have been recorded.

Though the Arctic and Antarctic Circles enclose the true polar regions, polar climates are experienced in many other areas of earth. Snow climates are places that receive snowfall during the winter months. They lie between 35° and 70° latitude and cover much of the northern half of the globe. The most hazardous snow climate is the area known as the continental subarctic (60–70° latitude). It features wild temperature swings throughout the year from –40°C in the winter to +40°C in the summer. Below this is the humid continental zone (35 to 60° latitude). This has a temperate climate and less dramatic temperature swings, but is still prone to severe and snowy winters.

For anyone in a subzero environment the immediate priority, above food and water, is the need for shelter and warmth. The wind-chill factor in freezing climates increases the physical impact of still-air temperature. For example, a temperature of 5°F (–14°C) becomes –30°F (–34°C) in a 20mph (32km/h) wind. Anyone exposed to severe wind-chill without sophisticated survival clothing will suffer from hypothermia and frozen body parts in a matter of minutes. A wind-chill temperature of –65°C (-80°F) will flash-freeze human tissue in 30 seconds. Consequently, finding or making shelter is the utmost priority, and after this comes food and water.

FINDING WATER

In most subzero environments, finding water is rarely a problem. Snow and ice are usually abundant and can be melted down for drinking water. However, dehydration is almost as much of a risk in polar regions as in the hottest deserts. Despite their snowy appearance, polar landscapes actually have very dry climates. Antarctica, for example, is actually the world's driest continent, with only 5–6in (12–15cm) of precipitation every year. There are even some snowless, rocky valleys in the Antarctic that scientists estimate have seen no rain or snow for two million years.

In subzero temperatures, all water moisture is frozen out of the air. When you breathe in this climate, you expel water moisture from your body – hence the cloud your breath forms on the air – but no moisture is taken back in. This unequal exchange means that dehydration can hit quite quickly in arctic conditions. Dehydration in turn

increases the risk of hypothermia. Therefore, as in deserts, set up a regular ration of water commensurate with your levels of exertion. Try to drink about 1 pint (0.5 litre) of water every two to three hours; more if you are involved in heavy activity.

In terms of fresh drinking water, snow and ice are the obvious source. In almost all circumstances melt the snow and ice down to water before drinking it. Eating ice and snow in their 'raw' state will increase the loss of body heat and may push you towards hypothermia. In addition, ice particles can cause damage to the mouth and lips by freezing the skin tissue.

The best way to melt snow and ice is by using a melting machine. Build a tepee-like structure out of the three branches or poles tied together at the top. Within the frame hang a piece of material like a bag to hold the snow and ice. Place a container to catch water on the base of the frame. By making a fire near to the melting machine, the snow and ice will melt and water will flow through the cloth and drip down into the container. The water extracted from snow and ice can, in most cases, be drunk without purifying. The exceptions to this rule are ice taken from around open seawater, as this may contain harmful marine micro-organisms, and ice near any industrial units (surprisingly common in polar regions).

Icebergs offer huge amounts of ice, but not all of it suitable for melting and drinking. Icebergs are composed of two types of ice. The first is ice from recently frozen seawater. This type is pure white, hard and glassy, and contains high levels of sea salt and so is unsuitable for melting into drinking water. The second type is ice that has aged and, in the process, lost its salt content and has become drinkable. This is blue or black in colour, and it is more fragile than saltwater ice, shattering easily under a blow from any hacking tool. Select ice from a side of the iceberg that is sheltered from the wind, as

Creating an ice melting device

To melt a large block of ice, first construct a stone platform set on four other large rocks. The gap beneath this platform should be sufficient to build a fire in, and the platform should slope down to one end. Once a fire is made beneath the platform, an ice block is placed on the hot stone slab and the melt-water runs off the lower end into a container.

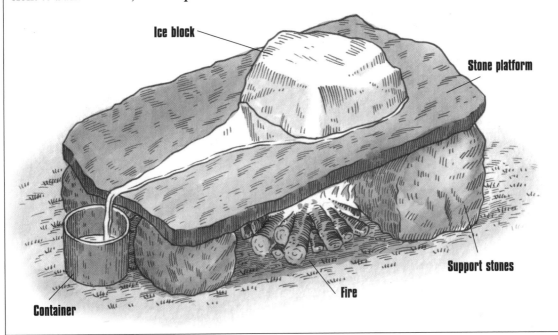

Ice block

Stone platform

Support stones

Fire

Container

winds will whip seawater spray against the ice and leave it with a heavy coating of salt.

Icebergs will provide fresh water in large quantities, but there are dangers. Only use icebergs that have lodged themselves firmly against a solid seashore or ice platform, not those surrounded by slopping, freezing seawater or shifting pack ice. When hacking off chunks of ice, do not dislodge any ice-blocks above, for icebergs regularly fracture and shed large sections, some of which weigh hundreds of tons. Icebergs are also prone to rolling over if unbalanced by any additional weight, so try to cut off ice without standing on the iceberg itself.

Amongst the Arctic landmasses, open water is easily found in the summer months.

On the tundra and in forested areas, melting snow and ice form lakes and rivers of fairly fresh water. Though the water is often coloured brown by vegetation and sediment, it will be some of the purest open water to be found anywhere in the world. Allow the water to stand in a container until all the silt has separated out and sunk to the bottom. The water can then, generally, be drunk without purification, though if the water is still cloudy, purification is recommended.

Storing water in arctic conditions is best done in a plastic water bottle. Metal water bottles tend to split if the contents freeze, whereas plastic stretches with the expansion of the ice. Nevertheless, do not fill water bottles up to the very top, but leave a gap for the ice to expand into. Wear a water bottle inside a coat if at all possible to stop it refreezing, as melting the water again and again consumes time and energy that is best spent on other survival matters.

FIRE AND COOKING

While making a melting machine is straightforward, making the fire necessary to make it work can be extremely difficult in polar climates. On ice sheets and glaciers, there is a total lack of burnable vegetation, while in the milder subarctic regions, everything that is burnable is usually soaked with snow.

In any survival emergency in polar climates, anything combustible must be salvaged immediately. Following a plane crash, explore the wreckage (once you have ensured that there is no risk of fire or explosion) and strip out any flammable materials. Sometimes aviation fuel will have soaked into the ground, and can be collected as a solid fuel. A broken-down vehicle also provides firelighting materials. Drain the oil from the sump while the vehicle is still warm – if it goes cold, the oil will congeal and become too viscous to remove (petrol/gasoline can be left in the tanks). Check seashores regularly for driftwood, which can be found in quite large quantities in the Arctic thanks to the refuse washed up from the northern shipping lanes.

In ice climates, one of the best burnable materials is actually animal fat. Seals and whales contain large amounts of flammable blubber that burns and gives off enough heat for cooking. When skinning a seal, cut away any fat and store it in a separate container for fire-making. On the arctic landmasses, there are a variety of plants that are useful for making fire, despite the snow. Select resinous woods that will burn even when wet. Birch, juniper, willow and pine branches make good fuel in this regard, especially if they are feathered to release their oils and provide more combustible surfaces. The bark of these

Making snowshoes

Find two long flexible saplings (willow is best) and trim them of any branches or uneven parts (A). Sharpen the ends of the saplings to provide extra heel grip to the shoe (B). Bend

A

the sapling into a balloon shape and knot the two ends firmly together (C). Tie double cross-members across the shoe frame, using short stout sticks (D). These cross-members should brace the foot in at least three positions: ball of foot, arch of foot, and heel (E). Add support wires and other struts if necessary to build up the shoe, then tie it securely to the foot.

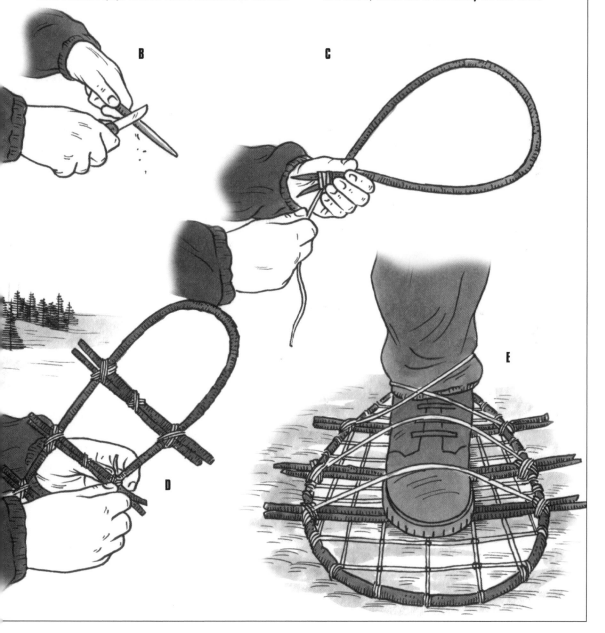

trees can be cut into strips for kindling. The Eskimos use a plant called casiope for fuel. It has the appearance of heather, is low-lying (between 4in/10cm and 12in/30cm in height) and evergreen, and can be identified by its tiny leaves and white bell-shaped flowers. It is highly resinous and is an ideal fuel for burning in wet climates.

Fires in snowy conditions should be built upon platforms to raise them above meltwater as the snow around them is warmed. These platforms can be made of either green wood or rocks, and should be sheltered from severe winds and snows by rocks, trees or snow ramparts.

HUNTING AND EATING ANIMALS

Simply moving in polar conditions, let alone hunting, is always difficult and treacherous. One of the greatest dangers is the possibility of getting lost in the featureless expanses of ice and snow. If there is a blizzard or heavy snow or winds, it is better to wait and hunt later when conditions have improved. When going out, leave highly visible markers at regular stages on your journey, and use these to find your way back to your shelter or camp.

Walking over snow and ice is exhausting, even in fair conditions. You can speed things up by making a pair of snowshoes. Take a green sapling several feet/metres long and bend it back on itself, tying the ends together firmly. Fit wooden crosspieces and twine across this frame, building up a more solid central section for your foot. Tie the snowshoes directly onto your boot. Make them easy to untie, however, in case you have to adopt a crawl when stalking.

Hunting across ice fields presents unique dangers. Plates of ice shift and crush together, suddenly pushing up ridges of ice at steep angles and opening up gaps into the freezing seawater in other places. Observe the patterns of ice movement closely. In particular, take care not to get stranded on a sheet of ice that is detaching itself from the whole.

Despite the obstacles, Arctic climates have certain advantages for the hunter. Animal tracks are clearly visible on the snow – the sharp impressions helping you to identify the creature. Camouflage for tracking an animal up close has to be made rather than found because of the flatness of the landscape. A bank of snow, positioned downwind from a creature, is a good 'hide' from which to launch a sudden attack with a projectile weapon. Alternatively, a piece of white cloth mounted on a frame will provide more mobile camouflage.

Falling into freezing waters

A fall into freezing water is one of the greatest dangers facing a polar survivor. Just the shock of hitting the water can precipitate a heart attack. Ice surrounding the water is especially slippery, and stops the person climbing out easily. Someone trapped in polar water will suffer from frozen body parts in four minutes, unconsciousness within seven minutes and death in about 20 minutes.

As soon as you hit the water, instantly strike out for the nearest solid surface. If this is ice, try to swim up it at speed, or use a knife or ski poles to claw your way out. Once on dry land, roll yourself in the snow to absorb excess water, then get to shelter straight away. Change into dry clothes within minutes of falling into freezing water, or the water in your clothing will freeze solid.

So severe is the true polar climate that few animals are capable of surviving, but there are enough to sustain survival.

Seals

Seals, the main component of the Eskimo diet, are found on coastlines and pack ice. Between March and June, they give birth to their pups. Because these pups are unable to swim or move quickly, they are easily caught by the survivor. A simple blow to the head with a club is enough to dispatch one. Adults are more difficult to catch, and tend to slip into the water before you reach striking distance. You can, however, use this fact against them by staking out air holes. Being mammals, seals need to take in air when swimming. To do so, they carve out cone-shaped holes in sheet ice and return to them about once every 7–15 minutes to snatch a breath. Wait by the hole. As soon as the seal's head emerges, club it, then widen the hole to retrieve the floating body. When butchering the seal, remove its fat straight away before it goes rancid and spoils the meat. Save this fat for fuel and do not eat the liver, which contains dangerous concentrations of vitamin A.

Walruses

Walruses grow to enormous sizes – an adult male can be

Arctic clothing from animal skins

The skins of polar animals make excellent survival clothing. To prepare the skin, first scrape away any fat or tissue from the flesh side of the skin. Next stretch the hide over a frame and allow to dry. Finally, smoke the hide over a fire to toughen it and make it more waterproof. Soaking a skin in a mix of warm water and animal brains will soften the hide to produce buckskin.

as much as 12ft (3.6m) long and weigh over two tonnes (tons), with tusks that can grow to 1m (3.25ft) in length. They are very violent and aggressive. For these reasons, it is best to leave walruses alone unless you are using a high-powered rifle.

Polar Bears

Polar bears are not a food option for most hunters. They are powerful killers and move fast over land and in water, and they live in the most inaccessible regions of the Arctic. Their sense of smell and their eyesight far exceed human capabilities, and they may well pursue a human who has wandered into their territory, especially if they have cubs. As with walruses, do not hunt them with anything other than a rifle, ideally one fitted with a telescopic sight so that you can use it from a safe distance. If you do manage to kill a polar bear, boil the muscle meat to destroy the trichinosis worms that are com-

mon to this animal. Do not eat the animal's liver because it contains Vitamin A in lethal concentrations.

Grazing animals

Subarctic forested regions are inhabited by several species of grazing animal, including caribou, musk ox and elk. Hunting these creatures is similar to hunting deer. Stalk them silently and despatch with a projectile weapon. Because of their large size it is best to use a gun, though a powerful bow and arrow may also work. Caribou are in the habit of investigating strange sights, which is useful to the hunter. Waving a flag on a stick may actually bring the creature over to you. The stomach contents of caribou contain fermented lichens, which can be eaten for extra nutrition.

Foxes and wolves

The arctic fox is a small creature that grows up to 22in (55cm) in length, excluding its tail. Its coat changes with the seasons: in summer it is reddish-brown, and in winter it turns the purest white. These exceptionally alert animals are difficult to hunt, so it is better to trap them. Arctic foxes prey on rabbits and other small burrowing creatures, so place snares at the mouths of burrows or outside the fox's den itself. When tracking an arctic fox, bear in mind that they often follow polar bears, hoping to scavenge the bear's kills.

Arctic fox

Wolves are stronger and larger creatures than foxes. They are usually present in the vicinity of caribou, preying on the weak and young members of the herd. Stay hidden and watch the caribou until the wolves strike in a pack. Then, if possible, despatch one with a projectile weapon while it is distracted with the kill. Wolves can also be trapped along hunting routes through forests.

Hares and small rodents

The subarctic and arctic climates are home to various small mammals, including arctic hares, lemmings, mink, stoats, squirrels and weasels. Catch these using snares or dead-falls positioned outside burrows or along routes littered with animal tracks. For carnivorous creatures, bait the traps with small pieces of meat. Note that arctic rodents can pass the disease tularaemia to humans simply through contact. Wear gloves when skinning these animals and boil the flesh to eat. Marmots are another good food source in mountainous areas. Their burrows are marked by large patches of orange lichen outside the entrance.

Beaver

Beavers betray their presence through the chewed and cut branches that they use to build their lodges. Set a large snare trap in the area in which the beaver is working or swimming. An underwater trap may be more effective than one on land. Find a point where the beaver enters and exits the water, and set the trap just beneath the waterline. A bundle of poplar or willow twigs make good bait. As with all traps in polar regions, check an underwater trap regularly to stop ice forming on it, which will affect its effectiveness.

Birds

The northern forests and tundra are inhabited by many different birds, which usually confine themselves to swampy and watery regions. They include grouse, cranes, owls, geese, swans, ptarmigans and ducks. Because many of these birds seldom see humans, they can be very approachable. Try walking slowly and unthreateningly up to one and then

Ptarmigan

either kill it with a throwing stick or stone at close range, or hit it with a club. Once every year during the summer, many arctic birds will suffer a moult that renders them flightless for two to three weeks. This is an excellent time for hunting them. In the Antarctic, penguins are another flightless food option.

Fish

Polar waters are usually rich in marine life. Edible fish types include the arctic cod and tom cod, eelpout, sculpin, grayling, trout, salmon and crayfish. Most of these can be caught either by traditional line and hook or by ice fishing. Shellfish are abundant, though mainly in subarctic regions. King crabs come close to the shore in spring and can be caught with a line. Mussels are exposed on rocks when the tide recedes, but never eat any that are not covered by the water during high tide. Also reject any that are dead when you find them – live mussels should close up when touched. To cook mussels, boil them for about 5–15 minutes, preferably in a container with a tight lid. When thoroughly cooked, the shells should have opened to reveal the mussel inside. If any haven't opened, reject them. Black mussels require special care and should be avoided if possible. If there is no choice but to eat them, select those that live in deep inlets and do not eat the poisonous black meat, only the white meat.

Obviously, meats are easily frozen in sub-zero conditions. Try to freeze them only in their raw state and then heat up only once to cook. Do not keep reheating meat as this results in the fibres disintegrating and increases the possibility of the food going off. For this reason, cut up all meats into

Ice fishing

To fish through sheet-ice, first cut a circular hole through the ice to reveal the water beneath. Bait a fishhook and attach the line to the end of a stick. Attach a piece of material to the other end of the stick as a pennant. Tie this pennant-stick at a right angle to another stick that is longer than the ice hole is wide. Lay this long stick by the edge of the

ice hole, and the pennant-stick flat to the ground with its line end over the centre of the hole (A). The principle behind ice fishing is that should a fish bite on the line, it will pull down on the pennant-stick and the flag will spring into the air, alerting you to the catch (B). The stick straddling the hole prohibits the fish's escape.

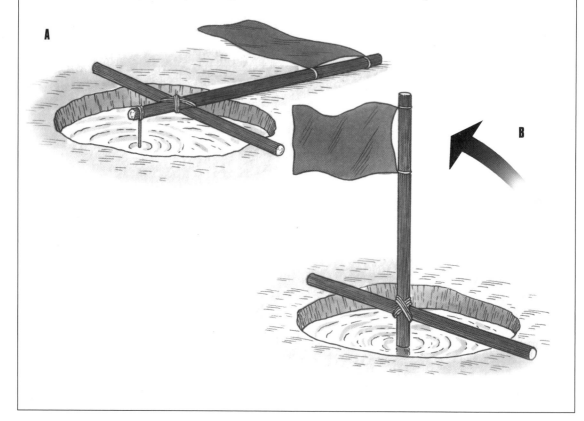

small, easily defrosted cubes. Use every part of the kill to aid other aspects of survival. Bones can be used for tools, fat for fuel and hide for clothing. Furs should be rolled up as soon as they are removed to make them easier to carry if they freeze.

Whatever animal you are hunting, look after your weapons in the subzero climate. Clean guns regularly but do not apply too much oil as it can freeze. Check that bolts, firing pins and ejector systems are free from ice and snow. Examine the barrel frequently to see that it is free of ice blockages that could cause a barrel explosion when the gun is fired. All metal weapons are prone to metal fatigue in polar conditions. Do not allow them to frost up and clean them regularly. One final safety note: avoid touching metal weapons or any other metal implement with your bare hands in freezing conditions. Your flesh will stick to the freezing metal and tear off when you pull your hand away.

PLANT FOOD

Ice sheets are almost utterly devoid of plant life, as there is no soil for rooting plants. Edible plant forms do, however, grow in rocky polar and subarctic regions. Some tenacious varieties of lichen and moss are found clinging to rocks, while in the summer, many temperate species are in evidence in the tundras and forests.

Edible Arctic and subarctic plants

Name: Alpine smartweed (*Polygonum viviparum*)
Description: Slender arctic perennial with pale pink or white flowers. Purple or red bulblets. Fleshy rootstock.
Eating notes: Bulblets can be eaten raw when stripped of flower heads. Rootstocks are eaten raw, boiled or roasted.

Name: Arctic willow (*Salix*)
Description: Mat-forming shrub growing to 2ft (0.6m) tall. Rounded shiny leaves and yellow catkins.
Eating notes: Edible shoots, leaves (very high in vitamin C), inner bark and roots (when peeled).

Name: Black crowberry (*Empetrum nigrum*)

Identifying poisonous Arctic plants

Most arctic plants are edible, but there are several poisonous varieties. Water hemlock/spotted cowsbane is by far the worst. This tall, common plant grows to about 4ft (1.3m) with a smooth, purple-streaked stem and clusters of small white flowers. A single mouthful of any part can kill. Monkshood, a smaller plant with helmet-like flowers and buttercup-like leaves, has a similar poisonous content. Some poisonous arctic plants need to be eaten in larger quantities before fatal results occur. These include the spring larkspur, an erect plant spurred with blue or white flowers and five- or seven-lobed leaves, and the more robust false hellesbore, with disproportionately large leaves and clusters of star-shaped yellow-green flowers.

A deceptive species to avoid is the wild lupine. This has blue or purple flowers that look like peas, and palm-shaped leaves. In the past, some survival texts have recommended the flowers as pea substitutes. However, they actually contain an alkaloid poison. Similarly, never eat the white or red berries of any species of baneberry, however appetizing they look.

Bearberry

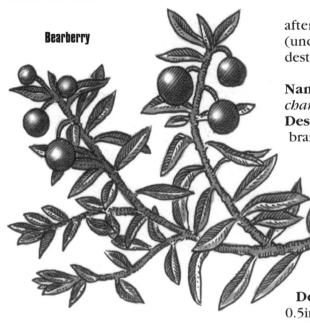

Description: Mat-forming shrub featuring tiny pink flowers and needle-like leaves. Pea-sized black berry July to November.
Eating notes: Fruit edible raw.

Name: Bearberry (*Arctostaphylos uva-ursi*)
Description: Low shrub with reddish bark and paddle-shaped evergreen leaves. Pink or white flowers and red berries.
Eating notes: Berries edible raw, but more palatable when cooked.

Name: Black spruce (*Picea mariana*)
Description: Smaller than red spruce with shorter needles and cones
Eating notes: Treat as Red Spruce.

Name: Bracken (*Pteridium acquilinum*)
Description: Very common fern, 1–6ft (0.3–1.8m) high.
Eating notes: Eat only young fiddleheads

after boiling them for 30–45 minutes (uncooked plant contains enzyme that destroys vitamin B).

Name: Cloudberries (*Rubus chamaemorus*)
Description: Small herbaceous plant with bramble-like appearance. Stems topped by single white flower accompanied by two or three five-lobed leaves. Berries go from peach to amber-yellow.
Eating notes: Berries can be eaten raw.

Name: Ground juniper (*Juniperus communis*)
Description: Flat shrub with needles 0.5in (1.3cm) long. Small blue-black berries with whitish covering.
Eating notes: Berries can be eaten raw, or crushed and added to meats for flavouring.

Name: Iceland moss (*Cetraria islandica*)
Description: Forms tufted olive-green to brown mats 1–3in (2.5–7.5cm) high. Strap-

Arctic Willow

like branches with tiny spines along the edges.
Eating notes: Soak thoroughly then boil to eat.

Name: Red spruce (*Picea rubens*)
Description: Steeple-shaped evergreen tree, 60–70ft (18–21m) high. Dark green or yellow-green needles 1.3cm (0.5in) long
Eating notes: Eat the tender shoots raw or cooked. Infuse the needles with hot water to make a tea. Inner bark can be boiled and eaten or dried and ground into meal.

Name: Reindeer moss (*Cladonia rangiferina*)
Description: Lichen named after its antler-like stems and branches. Grey and silver-grey in colour. Grows in large colonies
Eating notes: Soak for 3–4 hours, then boil. When dried, moss can be ground up and used as a flour.

Name: Rock tripe (*Umbillicaria*)
Description: A grey or olive-brown lichen that attaches to rocks in a blister-like fashion. 1–8in (2.5–20cm) wide. Brittle in dry state; leathery when wet.
Eating notes: Pre-soak for several hours, then simmer for about one hour to reduce acid content.

Name: Salmonberry (*Rubus spectabilis*)
Description: Similar appearance to wild raspberry. Three-section leaves and purple-red flowers. Red or yellow berries.
Eating notes: Berries can be eaten raw.

A selection of these plants, coupled with some of the meat sources listed above, are sufficient to ensure the full range of nutrition in a polar climate.

Storing food in an Arctic shelter

Arctic shelters can become surprisingly warm inside, which hastens the deterioration of food. Place food in a dedicated sump in the floor of the shelter near the shelter's entrance passage. The cold air from the entrance will keep the food chilled while the warm air from fires rises above floor level.

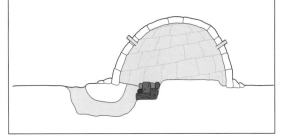

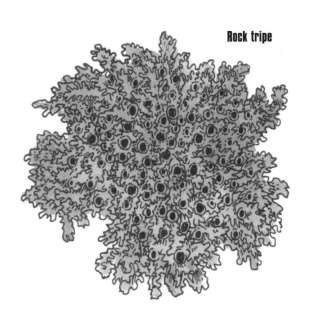

Rock tripe

CHAPTER NINE

Surviving in the tropics

Tropical areas have an abundance of survival foods and water. The main concerns for the survivor are avoiding disease, correctly identifying edible plants amongst poisonous ones, and coping with the jungle's wildlife.

Tropical rainforests and jungles are hostile places, with disease rife amongst indigenous peoples. Many of the world's most poisonous animals and plants are to be found there. Moving through the terrain and climate is exhausting. It is ironic, therefore, that the tropics are actually one of the easiest environments in which to survive. Everything needed for survival is there in abundance. Nutritious food, fresh water, and the materials for making fire and shelter are easily accessible. As long as dangerous flora and fauna are avoided, and health and hygiene rules rigorously obeyed, most people can meet the challenge of living in the jungle.

THE TROPICAL ENVIRONMENT

Tropical jungles have fairly predictable climates. Temperatures drop as altitude increases – tropical mountains over 4953ft (1500m) do experience freezing nights – but daytime temperatures at sea level are usually around 98°F (37°C). The oppressive heat combines with an 80–90 per cent humidity that makes the atmosphere damp and musty.

Jungles are usually classified according to three types: rainforests, secondary jungle and swampland. Each presents its own set of survival challenges and opportunities.

Rainforests

The common characteristic of rainforests is their consistently high rainfall, usually an annual deposit of 60–149in (1.5–3.5m). They are divided, however, into two sub-categories: equatorial rainforest and deciduous rainforest. The former are concentrated in the equatorial regions of the Amazon,

Indonesia, the Pacific and the Congo basin. Equatorial rainforests are a unique type of environment. A canopy of foliage formed by the upper leaves and branches of the jungle trees interlocks some 200ft (60m) above the jungle floor. This canopy is very dense and, consequently, the jungle floor exists in a strange, green twilight. Because of the limited light, foliage at ground level is minimal, which makes walking easier than in other types of jungle, and the temperatures cooler.

Deciduous rainforests are found in regions just off the equatorial line, usually within 10° of latitude. Unlike equatorial rainforests, which have fairly constant rainfall, deciduous jungles have cyclical patterns of violent rains - the monsoon - followed by long dry periods tantamount to drought. During these dry spells, foliage dies back, allowing sunlight to reach the jungle floor, stimulating dense plant growth. The monsoon season restores water to the land, but brings major problems for inhabitants and travellers. Torrential downpours turn the jungle into a muddy quagmire, rivers burst their banks, mudslides sweep away trees, and the mosquitoes become unbearable.

Secondary jungle

Secondary jungle occurs in an area of jungle that has been cleared - usually for slash-and-burn farming - then abandoned to nature once again. The re-growth is chaotic, and dense, with plants such as thorn bushes, dense shrubs, weeds and vines growing at a rate of up to 32ft (10m) a year. For the survivor, secondary jungle is one of the worst environments. Travel is tortuously slow and painful, visibility is often restricted to a few feet/metres, and the light levels are dim and gloomy.

Swamps

Tropical swamps are divided into saltwater and freshwater types. Saltwater swamps occur on coastlines and interact with the tides and waters of the sea, whereas freshwater swamps exist around inland waterways. The saltwater swamp - also known as a mangrove swamp because of the plant that thrives there - is a treacherous environment. Thick roots and dense vegetation choke the waterways above and below the waterline. Rafting is usually impossible. Instead, the survivor goes on foot through stagnating pools and foul mud, usually at a crawling pace, avoiding leeches, crocodiles and mosquitoes. The swamps are also tidal, and the waters can rise by as much as 40ft (12m) when the tide is in (you can judge the level they have risen by the salt deposits on the trees).

Freshwater swamps are less demanding than their saltwater cousins. Visibility, movement and hostile animal life still abound, but small, island-like patches of high ground provide havens for drying out clothes and wet skin. There is also more open, flowing water, so rafting is a viable method of travel.

THE THREAT OF DISEASE

In all types of jungle, the survivor faces some common enemies. The major problem is illness. The humidity and temperature of the tropics provides the perfect conditions for disease, bacteria and decomposition to thrive. Tropical regions are home to many fatal diseases, including diphtheria, tuberculosis, yellow fever, dengue, bacillary dysentery and leptospirosis to name but a few. Serious illnesses are spread by insects and parasites such as hookworm and mosquitoes (mosquito-borne malaria kills around 12 million people each year worldwide). Bacteria prey upon damp flesh, which results in maceration - the skin softens and begins to decay, usually in parts of the body where different patches of flesh rub together, for example armpits and the groin. Don't be too frightened, however, by these dangers. Millions of people do succumb to these illnesses, but mostly they are people made vulnerable by poverty. While heart disease, cancer and strokes are the number-one killers in the USA and the developed world, diarrhoeal illnesses, respiratory infections and malaria are their equivalent in tropical Africa, Asia and Latin America. Yet these tropical illnesses were present in the USA up until the early 1900s (cases of malaria were experienced as far north as the US–Canadian border). They were eventually eradicated by leaps in understanding about public health, accompanied by increased wealth and vastly improved standards of living. For travellers to tropical areas, the precautions are straightforward. Have all relevant vaccinations prior to travel (take advice from a doctor at least six months in advance of travel); avoid foods that have not been peeled or cooked (preferably by yourself); purify all water; wash in purified water; and do not eat local dairy products. Follow these rules, and your chances of contracting a fatal illness are minimal.

HEAT EXHAUSTION

A much more immediate danger in the jungle is heat exhaustion. When your body senses it is overheating, about 65 per cent of your body heat is radiated out into the atmosphere to help you cool down. However, when the atmosphere reaches around 95°F (35°C), the temperature at the body's core, simple physics dictates that your body cannot pass heat into an environment that is the same temperature or hotter. At this point, the body switches to evaporating sweat from the skin to try to keep itself cool. But in jungles, the very high humidity often means that the air is incapable of receiving the evaporated sweat particles. Instead, the sweat just runs off you, and has no cooling benefit. Once this occurs, heat exhaustion can set in with fatal results. Preventing tropical heat exhaustion requires acclimatization and adequate amounts of water. Adjust to the tropical environment at least two weeks before you do anything truly strenuous. Do, however, take light exercise to condition your body

to what lies ahead. Drink at least 1 pint (0.5 litre) of water every two hours when in the jungle and take salt regularly. If you are not carrying water or supplies are low, then you will have to look for natural sources of water.

WATER

Finding water is rarely a problem in jungles. Even during the dry season, the high annual rainfall means that open, underground and plant-stored water is easily found.

When dealing with open water, always filter and sterilize it before drinking. Streams and rivers in tropical regions will contain a large amount of decaying plant and animal matter. Also, impoverished local inhabitants tend to use open water for all sanitation and hygiene – it is not uncommon to see someone defecating into a stream only feet/metres away from someone using the same water for washing. Tropical water is a major disease carrier, but following the standard processes of filtering and sterilizing will make it safe to drink. You may need to repeat the filtering process more times than with temperate-zone waters because jungle waters contain large quantities of sediment. For this reason, you may find that a pump filter clogs up very quickly and needs regular filter changes.

If open water is not available, then water from plants is one of your best options. Care is needed when identifying plant types, as poisonous plants impart their poisons to the water. Do not take water from any plant with a milky or highly coloured sap or with water content that is similarly coloured. A well-known exception is, of course, the coconut.

When testing plants for hidden water, see if they are receiving regular visits from insects, particularly columns of ants. Mosquitoes and flies may also gather in swarms above the plant. The physical structure of the plant itself is a good guide to its water-holding potential. In tropical America, bromeliad plants store water at the point where their leaves gather together at the

Building a log raft

Wood from trees is possibly the most plentiful resource in jungle habitats but fashioning raw logs into a practical raft takes expertise. Follow the method below to find out how to do it quickly and simply.

(A) Find 12–14 logs, trim off any branches or other protrusions and cut to the same length. Cut out notches in the central portions of all the logs but leave about 1ft (30cm) at each end.

(B) Lay down two support logs on the floor with the carved faces upwards and make a

deck between them using the other logs. Interlock the notches of the guide logs and the deck logs.

(C) When the platform is constructed, place two more support logs, carved face down, over all the deck logs. Lash the top and bottom support logs firmly together, trapping the deck

logs tightly between them and stabilizing the whole structure.

(D) Finally, construct an elementary rudder and fit it to the aft of the raft using a flexible lashing. You should always test the raft in shallow water first before sailing on deeper rivers.

base. These plants grow up to 30ft (9m) high (though, more commonly, they reach 1–5ft/0.3–1.5m) and can provide a substantial drink of fresh water. Pitcher plants exist in several varieties throughout Southeast Asia, mainly in the more mountainous areas, but all have a leaf structure that effectively forms a large, upturned cup. The pitcher plant uses this water-filled cup to trap and digest insects, so boil any water obtained from this source. A larger water-collecting plant is the Ravenala madagascariensis, or traveller's tree. This palm-like tree holds water at the intersection of the leaf stalks. It is quite feasible to obtain 2–4 pints (1–2 litres) of drinkable liquid from this plant.

Rather than collecting water in open, accessible cup-like formations, some plants hold it inside themselves. Bamboo is an example that many people will be familiar with. Shake the bamboo stem. If you hear water sloshing around inside, cut a small hole just above each joint and pour the water out into a container. Vines, which are abundant in most jungle environments, also hold water inside. Learn in advance which vines are poisonous – they tend to have a milky white sap – or, at least, stop drinking from vines the instant you get any allergic reaction.

The stumps of banana and plantain trees are another good source of drinking water. Slice through the tree trunk about 12in (30cm) above the ground and then hollow out the stump to form a bowl with walls at 45° angles. Remove any bits of cut vegetation from the bowl, cover it with leaves, and then leave it for a few hours. Drinking water will seep from the wood and collect in the bowl.

Finally, palms provide drinking water from their flowering stalks. These stalks are found at ground level on the nipa palm, but, with the buri and coconut palms, some careful climbing may be required to reach them. Take one of these stalks and bend it so that its tip points downward. Then slice off the tip. It will begin to drip water. Keep

Using a pitcher plant

Pitcher plants can hold up to 8 pints (4 litres) of liquid depending on the species. However, the water is usually contaminated with dead insects (even dead rats have been reported) as the pitcher plant is carnivorous. About 100 species of pitcher plant also house live insects which manage to live within the plant's watery trap. All water taken from pitcher plants should be filtered and purified before drinking.

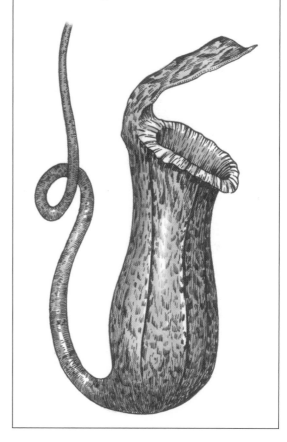

slicing the end off about twice a day to maintain the flow. Using this method, you will extract about 1 pint (0.5 litre) of water from the tree every two days. And, of course, you can also drink the milk of the coconuts. Don't try to smash the whole nut open with a blunt instrument. Instead, use a thin sliver of rock or a knife to puncture through the top and then drink from the hole. Once emptied, the coconut can be smashed open to reach the edible and nutritious flesh inside.

JUNGLE PLANT FOODS

There is no place on earth with greater bio-diversity than the tropical jungles. This is good news for the survivor because it means that food is abundant. The complication, though, is being able to identify poisonous species of plants. As ever, stick with clearly

Extracting water from a vine

To extract the water from a vine, sever it with a machete as high up its length as possible (A). Next chop off the bottom few inches of the cut section. With this last cut, water will begin to drip from the bottom of the vine; simply direct

the flow into your mouth or a bucket (B). If it stops dripping, cut another small section from the bottom to renew the flow. Remember always to sever vines from the top. If the order is reversed, a capillary action will draw the water further up into the plant, making it harder to retrieve.

Extracting water from a banana tree

Up to three days of water supply can be extracted from a large banana tree. Cut the tree down about 12in (30cm) above the ground (A), hollow out the stump and water will fill the stump after about two or three hours (B). Once the stump is drunk dry, cover it over with banana leaves and allow to refill. The banana leaves prevent insects taking the water and slow evaporation.

identifiable plants such as palms, bamboos and fruits – and use the universal edibility test to determine whether a plant is edible when there is any doubt.

When hunting for plant food, follow rivers, streams and other watercourses if possible. These are usually sunnier places than the jungle floor and so encourage fresh and varied plant growth. Spotting edible plants while sailing down the river on a raft can also be a quicker way of gathering food than struggling along on foot. Elevated ridges and rocky outputs often afford spectacular views out over the jungle canopy, from which you can spot plants and trees with edible parts. Palms, for example, stand out clearly from the mass of trees because of their distinctive fronds.

There is much plant food to be found in the jungle, so take only what you need – anything else will start to decay rapidly.

Edible jungle plants

Name: Nipa palm (*Nifpa fruticans*)
Description: Large leaves with fern-like appearance. Leaves gather at bottom to form trunk just above ground. Grows up to 19.6ft (6m).
Eating notes: Sweet, thick edible sap and excellent fruit.

Name: Banana or plantains (*Musa*)
Description: Up to 30ft (10m) tall with large, tough, leathery leaves. Distinctive 'feathered' trunk. Very common throughout the tropics.
Eating notes: Familiar banana fruit can be eaten raw; plantain fruit requires boiling or roasting. Other edible parts include stems of young plants and the inside of roots.

Name: Coconut palms (*Cocos nucifera*)
Description: Easily identified by clusters of nuts high up. Grows to 90ft (30m) high.
Eating notes: Nuts contained within a green husk that has to be split open. The inside of the coconut can be used for its milk and flesh. Avoid drinking too much milk as it can cause diarrhoea.

Wild figs

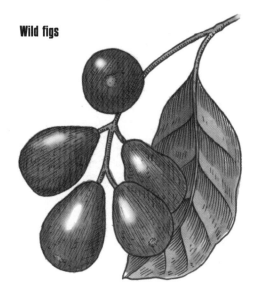

Name: Papaya (*Carica papaya*)
Description: Tree between 6.5ft (2m) and 18ft (6m) tall. Large fruit that ripens from green, through to orange or yellow. Hollow trunk.
Eating notes: Fruit edible raw (avoid getting any sap from unripe fruit in the eyes as it produces a burning pain). Boil young leaves, stems and flowers.

Name: Mango (*Mangifera indica*)
Description: Grows in moist areas. Oval fruit up to 5in (13cm) in diameter; ripens from green to orange.
Eating notes: Fruit is edible raw.

Name: Fig (*Ficus*)
Description: Tree with roots above the ground and rounded evergreen leaves. Pear-shaped fruits.
Eating notes: Fruit is edible raw.

Name: Bael fruit (*Aegle marmelos*)
Description: Tree reaching to 15ft (4.5m). Thorny spikes on branches. Round yellow or grey fruits about 4in (10cm) across.
Eating notes: Fruits edible raw.

Name: Goa beans (*Psophocarpus*)
Description: A climbing plant with blue flowers and spear-like leaves. Brown seed pods about 8in (20cm) long.
Eating notes: Leaves can be eaten raw. Seed pods should be boiled and eaten whole. Roast seeds if they have aged. Roots are eaten raw or cooked and are very high in protein.

Name: Peanut (*Arachis hypogaea*)
Description: Small bush with recognizable wrinkled brown pods containing the peanuts. Yellow flowers.
Eating notes: Eat nuts raw. High in fat and protein.

Name: Wild yams (*Dioscorea*)

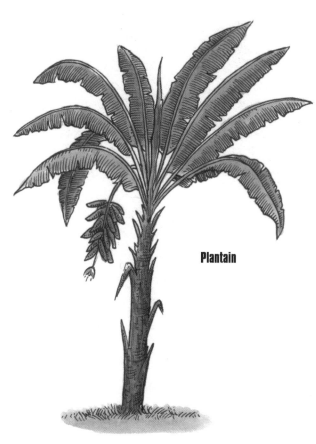

Plantain

Description: Vine-like plant often wrapping around other vegetation.
Eating notes: Edible tubers above and below ground. Always peel and boil (some uncooked Yams are poisonous). Mash to eat.

Name: Sweet Potato (*Ipomoea*)
Description: Vine-like plant with heart-shaped leaves. Large edible tubers like elongated potatoes.
Eating notes: Boil or roast the tubers.

The plants listed above are common throughout most tropical regions, but there are hundreds more that can be used for survival food. When learning about tropical foodstuffs, pay equal attention to identifying poisonous plants, especially the following:

Peanut

Castor Oil Plant (*Ricinus communis*); Cowhage (*Mucuna pruriens*); Duchnesia (*Duchnesia indica*); Nettle Trees (*Laportea*); Pangi (*Pangium edule*); Sandbox Tree (*Hua crepitans*); Strychnine (*Strychnox nuxvomica*); White Mangrove (*Avicennia marina*).

ANIMAL FOODS

Acquiring animal foods in the jungle is complicated by two factors: 1) movement is often slow, noisy and treacherous; and 2) the tropics have a far higher percentage of dangerous animals than temperate zones. Learning proper techniques of jungle movement makes hunting more efficient and safer.

When moving down jungle trails, try to keep up a steady and rhythmic pace. At first you stumble and fall many times, but simply pick yourself up and try to return to the rhythm. By keeping to this rhythm, movement through the jungle becomes more fluid and confident, and greater distances are travelled in less time. When you do fall, do not reach out with your hands to catch hold of plants. Many plants in the jungle are protected by spiny barbs, sharp leaves or penetrating thorns. Grabbing one of these may result in a punctured, lacerated or infected hand. Instead of grabbing, simply fold up and drop to the ground. This is not a natural

Making a bamboo cooking pot

A simple cooking pot, ideal for boiling vegetables and meat, can be made in minutes out of a section of bamboo. First, cut out a large, cylindrical section of bamboo, the cuts falling just outside the joints. In the centre of the section, cut out a small rectangular opening by making four incisions through the surface and then running a machete between them. Pop out the resulting 'plug'. Support the section of bamboo on forked sticks, with the opening facing upwards. Water and foodstuffs can be added through the opening, and a fire built beneath the bamboo 'pot' for convenient cooking.

reaction, so practise it in a safe place first until it becomes second nature.

A machete must be part of your kit, as it is vital to effective travel through thick undergrowth. Look after it, keep it greased to protect it from rust and sharpen it regularly. When hacking through undergrowth, slice down at an angle to split the vegetation. Never chop at a right angle to the plant, which will result in a trapped blade. Don't slash haphazardly, but cut in a rhythmic motion, and be careful if your are cutting very wet vegetation, as this increases the chances of the machete flying out of your hand. It is a good idea to bind the grip hand in cloth to protect it from the lacerations caused by sawgrass. These lacerations are small and might not be noticed at first, but they can result in very painful infections.

Jungle hunting often depends on hearing before sight. Native hunters will stand silently in the jungle, listening for prey and rocking their head gently to one side to improve their sense of direction. Once they have pinpointed the sound, they then rely on their eyes. In low light or night-time conditions, eyesight relies more on peripheral vision than direct line of sight. A silhouetted figure against a dark background will seem to disappear if looked at directly. When hunting in these conditions, look at the outline of the prey rather than focusing on its centre to get a clearer sight, and keep your eyes moving.

Edible animal life is plentiful in the jungle.

Insects are everywhere on the jungle floor and in the foliage. Birds, primates and lizards inhabit the trees, while small species of deer and wild pigs will often be found rooting around at ground level. Take advantage of the diversity on offer by mixing hunting with trapping. Jungle animal trails are quite well defined and are used by many species because they are convenient for travel. Consequently, they make ideal sites for setting traps. Be careful though – such tracks are often used by indigenous peoples, so never set any traps where there are human footprints or human habitation close by.

EDIBLE JUNGLE ANIMALS

Tapirs

Tapirs are tropical herbivorous creatures found throughout most of Southeast Asia and South America. They are similar in appearance to pigs, apart from an unusual rubbery mouth, and can be very large – the Malayan Tapir, for example, grows up to 8.25ft (2.5m) and can weigh 1190lb (540kg). Tapirs are nocturnal animals and in the daytime are frequently found sleeping in thick undergrowth on the edge of swampland. Despite their slumber, be very quiet as you approach. If alerted, they execute a fast dive into the water and it is doubtful that you will catch them. Kill them with a gun, a deep penetrating strike from a spear or a crushing blow to the head with a club or stone.

Chevrotain

Chevrotain, or mousedeer, live in central and western Africa and in south Asia, particularly India and Malaysia. They are the world's smallest deer – some of the Indian species are only around 20in (50cm) long in the body. Like all deer, they are edgy, sensitive prey, but they are susceptible to the old hunter's trick of lamping. Hunt in the dark with a torch. When you see one of the deer, shine the torch directly into the creature's eyes. It will often stand transfixed by the glare long enough for you to stride forward and despatch it with a club.

Capybara

The Capybara is a large rodent that grows up to 4.25in (1.6m) in length and can weigh up to 145lb (66kg). Its habitat is swamps, rivers and lakes throughout South America, and it is an excellent swimmer and diver. All hunting efforts should be focused on catching it on the banks. Indicators that a capybara is close are its distinctive grunts and squeals and its slightly webbed footprints in the mud. Try to kill with a projectile weapon at a distance, and be wary when approaching these creatures, as they can deliver nasty bites and scratches. These creatures are much prized by locals for their food and hide.

Monkeys

Monkeys are eaten by indigenous peoples throughout the tropical world. Tackle only the smaller varieties, though, and never large chimpanzees or gorillas, which can be extremely violent. As you travel through the jungle, note any colonies of monkeys and the routes they take through the trees. Monkeys can be either trapped or hunted with projectile weapons, but make sure that the means match the prey – monkeys are strong and aggressive when wounded. A wounded monkey will also scream at deafening volume, alerting other animals to its distress and attracting predators. Spear traps baited with fruit are particularly effective against monkeys, as are the preferred methods of many jungle communities – the blowpipe and the bow and arrow.

Termites

Termites are a nutritious and tasty supplement to a tropical survival diet. Nests of termites are large mud constructions up to 3–4ft (1–1.2m) high with a very tough outer shell. The easiest way to collect termites is to push a long, thin stick through a hole in the side of the nest. Adult termites will treat the stick as a hostile intruder and lock their jaws onto it. After a few seconds, withdraw the stick and scrape the clinging termites into a container. Termites can also be gathered by smashing a piece of the nest off with a stone and dropping it into water. The water will force the termites out of the honeycombed passages and they will float to the surface. Finally, flying termites are simply picked off

Wild pig

Silvery Gibbon

vegetation near the nest. Termites are best eaten raw to preserve their nutritional value, but, when cooking, remove wings and legs and boil, fry or roast.

FISH

Apart from land animals, fish are one of the best sources of meat to be found in the tropics. Fishing techniques are explored in full in the final chapter, but there are a couple of issues exclusive to tropical fishing, and one or two distinct methods.

Since many tropical diseases originate from water sources, try not to enter rivers and streams unless absolutely necessary, and protect yourself if you do so. Cover any open sores or wounds with waterproof plasters to protect against parasite intrusion. Always wear something on your feet to avoid puncture injuries. When emerging from the water, check for leeches attached to the skin. Do not pull them straight off – they attach themselves to flesh very firmly and, if yanked off,

How to make a blowpipe

The blowpipe has been the primary hunting weapon of jungle tribes for centuries, and has only recently been replaced by the gun. With the correct poison, blowpipes can bring down squirrels, wild boar, monkeys and birds. A simple blowpipe can be made out of any piece of hollow reed or bamboo, but an effective hunting version requires some basic tools. Blowpipes are fashioned from a piece of straight-grained wood about 6.5ft (2m) long and about

5.9in (15cm) in diameter. The bore of the weapon is drilled out, and native hunters of Borneo use a long piece of steel with a chisel-shaped end that is worked through the wood in a rotational motion. Water is poured into the hole to clear out pieces of cut wood. Once the hole is drilled right through, the diameter is pared down to about 2in (5cm), effectively creating a long barrel. Pieces of rattan are pulled through the inside of the bore to smooth it out.

The darts are made from

the split leaf stalks of trees such as the arenga palm. Thorns are used for the penetrating point and are coated with lethal poisons. One of the most common poisons is extracted from the sap of the Ipol tree (Antiaris toxicaria). This poison causes heart arrhythmia and can even cause the heart to stop beating, and will kill a large pig in minutes. Few people still use the blowpipe for hunting, but tribesmen in Borneo demonstrate the skill by hitting a single leaf at 50ft (15m).

they will leave their mouth behind to infect the wound. Instead, touch them with a naked flame or sprinkle them with salt to make them shrivel and fall off intact.

Tropical fishing finds a useful accomplice in the shape of poisonous tropical plants. Several types of plant poison are harmful to fish but not to humans. Released into the water, these poisons will quickly bring fish to the surface. Warmer water temperatures in the tropics also help the poison to diffuse through the water more quickly and aid its efficacy on contact.

The main poison you are looking for is called rotenone, and it can be found in the following plants:

Barringtonia
Tree that grows in tropical coastal regions. Grind up the seeds and bark of the tree and throw into the water.

Anamirta cocculus
An Asian and Pacific vine. Seeds should be crushed up and thrown into the water.

Croton tiglium
Small tree or shrub of the South Pacific islands. Crush the seeds and throw into the water.

Derris eliptica
Order of shrubs and vines. Grind up the roots and mix with water, leaving overnight if possible. Pour substance into the water the next day.

Protective clothing for insect gathering

When gathering stinging insects or disturbing their nests (such as when collecting honey), wear as much protective clothing as possible. Put on extra layers of clothing on both the torso and legs, wear gloves, put netting over the face and neck and tuck it into the collar. Use sticks inserted into the collar to raise the face netting away from the surface of the head so that insects cannot sting through. Elastic bands around the wrists and ankles stop the insects from invading the clothing.

Poisoning is a good way to bring up large quantities of fish, possibly more, in fact, than you can immediately eat. Any food in the tropics – plant or vegetable – will decay beyond edibility within hours if left untreated. Salting and smoking are probably the best ways of drying food, as the high humidity usually prohibits drying by air. Smoking has an added value in that the smoke keeps insects away from your camp area, and can make life a bit more bearable.

DANGEROUS CREATURES

There are more life-threatening creatures in the tropics than most places, but, by using common sense, they shouldn't cause too many problems for the hunter. Big cats such as tigers, jaguars and leopards, are usually rare or reclusive (often both). They will almost always steer clear of human beings. Isolated cases of attack are generally carried out by wounded or old creatures in need of easy prey. These attacks are confined to villages and waterways. If there are reports of attacks in an area, beware of long grasses, which are a common site for a big cat ambush. Far more worrying is the threat from crocodiles and alligators. Stay well clear of them, and be especially vigilant if you are at the water's edge – a crocodile can glide up to attack in total silence, with little more than his eyes showing above the water.

If you wander into human habitations, beware of indigenous guard dogs, which will often attack anyone who is unfamiliar. If the dog growls but wags its tail, it will probably not attack. If it goes very stiff with tail upright, shows its teeth and violently alternates between snarling and barking, then an attack is likely. Do not stare the animal in the eyes, as this is perceived as a threat. Instead, tilt your head downwards (a submissive posture) and very slowly retreat away from the animal without turning your back on it. Some evidence suggests imitating the whimpering sounds of a puppy, to bring out any maternal

Boomslang

or paternal instincts in the creature, is also an effective way of avoiding attack.

The greatest cause for concern for most people are the many poisonous creatures found in the tropics, particularly snakes, scorpions and spiders. Snakes are common in the jungle, and some have exceptionally lethal poisons. The worst culprits are the following:

Africa and Asia
Boomslang; cobras; kraits; mambas; puff adder; vipers (including Malay pit-viper, Russel's viper, and the saw-scaled viper)

Australasia
Australian black snake; death adder; sea snake; taipan

North and South America
Bushmaster; coral snakes fer de lance

Treat all snakes as poisonous unless positively identified otherwise. Snakes will rarely attack a human unless they are disturbed or threatened. Therefore, watch that you do not step inadvertently on a coiled snake (some have very good ground camouflage), and wear strong ankle boots just in case you do. When exploring trees and branches, check that snakes are not coiled around them. Use sticks to turn over stones and logs, never your hands. Examine bedding and clothing with a stick before getting into them, as snakes like to coil up in warm, dark places to sleep. Finally, if you do come face to face with a snake, move off very slowly without turning your back and allow the snake plenty of room to wriggle off. Any fear you might have of these creatures, however, should not stop you from pursuing them as food.

Similar precautions apply to scorpions and spiders. Very few arachnids are capable of killing an adult human, with the exception of the funnelweb or black widow (spiders) or buthids (scorpion). Most fatalities are still restricted to the young, old or sick. Avoid touching spider webs, and be especially careful when exploring under rocks and logs, and in rodent holes (which may actually be

Mamba

inhabited by spiders or scorpions). Knock out your boots before putting them on, as scorpions appreciate the darkness of a shoe as a good place to sleep.

There is a multitude of other dangers in the jungle. Some tropical centipedes and millipedes can give agonizing poisonous bites – if they land on you, brush them off in the direction they are walking. Vampire bats and mosquitoes feed off humans while they sleep – so keep covered and use insect repellent. Hornets can launch a lethal mass attack – so stay away from their nests.

The important point is not to let fear put you off jungle travel. Your vaccinations will take care of most tropical diseases, and there is very little chance of your being killed by an animal. With a sound knowledge of a small selection of plants and animals, living off the jungle, though it will never be exactly comfortable, is perfectly feasible.

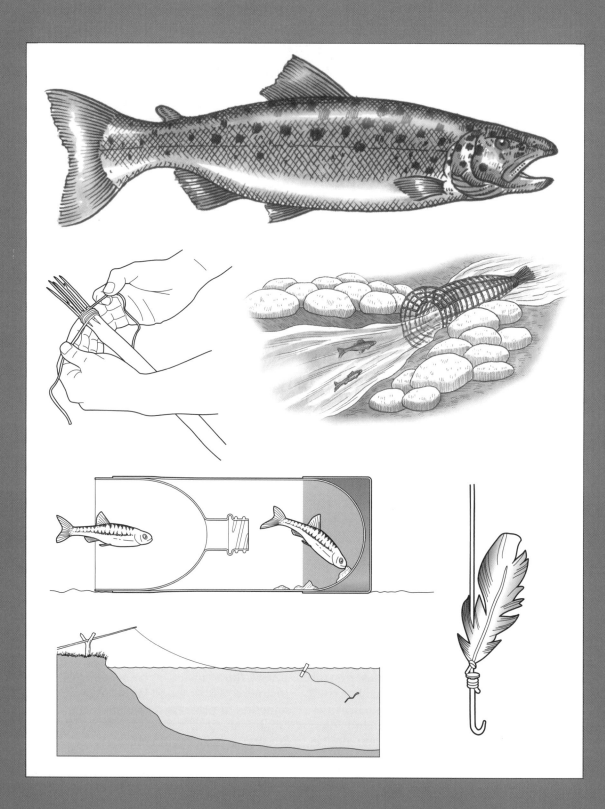

CHAPTER TEN

Surviving water environments

Fish provide more meat and protein weight-for-weight than land animals. Yet rivers, streams and seas provide many other foods which can keep a person alive.

Over 70 per cent of the earth's surface is covered by water. Mostly, this comprises the seas and oceans, rivers, streams, ponds and lakes that irrigate the temperate and non-arid tropical world. In terms of drinkable fluids and accessible food, the world's inland waters can meet almost all of a survivor's needs. Seas and oceans, however, are far more hazardous, their salt waters – home to many dangerous creatures – undrinkable unless treated.

FOODS ALONG COASTLINES

The foods that most people associate with water are fish and other swimming creatures, but the places where water intersects with the land are an excellent starting point for finding various kinds of edible vegetation. Seaweed, which is prevalent along shorelines, has great nutritional value, especially in its mineral content. It is usually found in clumps or mats clinging to rocky surfaces, but large amounts are also to be found floating in the open sea. The main types of common edible seaweed are:

Dulse
a short stem opens up into a dark-red fan, which wafts in the currents. Found on both sides of the Atlantic.

Irish Moss
a leathery, resilient seaweed. When dried it becomes crisp and brittle.

Kelp
found from arctic to tropical regions, usually on submerged rocks and ledges. It has a

short stem that branches out into olive-green or brown fronds.

Laver

a shiny, purple-red seaweed common to the Atlantic and Pacific oceans.

Though seaweeds are easily found, they should be eaten with caution They are very rich foods, which, if consumed in quantity, can lead to chronic diarrhoea. Eat only small quantities at a time and always boil to kill any parasites.

Plankton

A more unusual food from the seas, oceans and some inland waterways is plankton. Plankton consists of tiny plants and animals, particularly sea animals in the larval stage. Plankton floats around the oceans in enormous clouds, vast enough to form the staple diet of many of the world's largest sea creatures (including whales and basking sharks). It is a perfectly edible survival food with high levels of fats, proteins and carbohydrates. To catch it, simply drag a fine-mesh net through the water. Reject any plankton that are gelatinous or spiny, and also check your catch carefully for any jellyfish tentacles. Introduce yourself slowly to plankton. Eat only small quantities at first to acclimatize your digestive system, and always drink plenty of fresh water to help break down the proteins and fats.

Shellfish

Shellfish are probably the most accessible food of the seas and oceans. Rocky shores, for instance, are scattered with winkles and limpets. These can be prized from the rock with a knife, but only take those creatures that are difficult to remove. If they fall off too easily, it may mean that they are already dead. Mussels are found on the floor of rocky pools, while sandy beaches are home to razor shells, another good survival food. Razor shells dig a vertical tunnel down into the

Where to look for fish

As a survivor you would be confident that the features of this river suggest several likely locations of fish. The fallen tree and the overhanging branches attract fish which want to

Overhanging branches

Gravel bank

rest in the shade. Patches of floating weeds serve a similar purpose or draw fish which are feeding off the plant material. Gravel banks and large boulders create pools of still water just downstream in which fish might rest from swimming against fast currents.

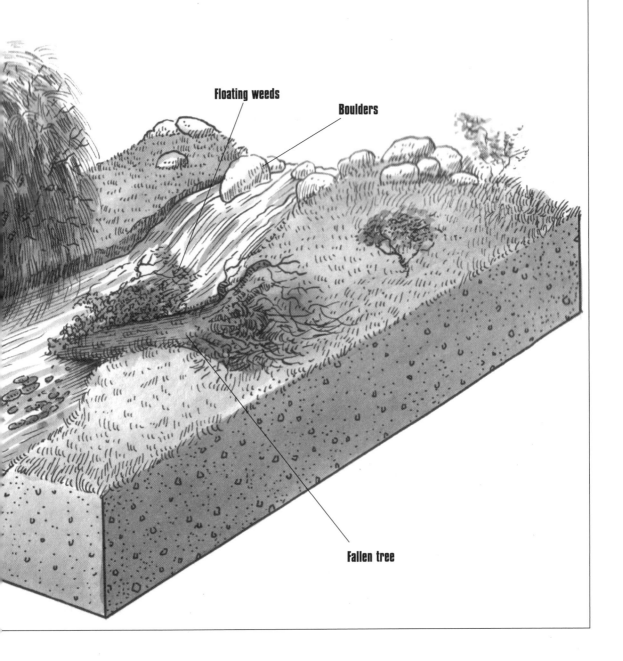

Floating weeds

Boulders

Fallen tree

Dangerous fish and sea creatures

Barracuda
Large fish (6.5ft/2m) that inhabits tropical and subtropical waters. It is aggressive, fast and has razor-sharp teeth. It is known to have attacked humans in murky waters when it confuses them for prey, and has also injured fishermen who attempt to spear it.

Bulhead
A type of catfish that inhabits freshwater rivers throughout Europe and North America. Its spines are coated with poison and its body is covered with poisonous mucus.

Electric eels
These large eels of South America can grow up to 7ft (2m) long and deliver an electric shock of 500 volts when threatened.

Piranhas
Piranhas can grow up to 20in (50cm) long. They are found throughout the major river systems of South America and will attack humans with their razor-sharp teeth if other foods are scarce, particularly during periods when water levels are low.

Rabbitfish
This black, white and yellow fish of Indo-Pacific waters grows up to 9.5in (24cm) in length, and has poisonous fin spines.

Sharks
Sharks will rarely attack humans if left alone, though may do so if the humans are mistaken for prey or the sharks are in a feeding frenzy around a kill. If the shark circles several times around a person, it is more likely to attack.

Stingrays
Dangerous varieties of stingray are prevalent in tropical waters. They tend to inhabit the shallows, covering themselves with sand. They are difficult to spot and, if stepped on, can inject poisons through venomous spines on their tail. These injuries can be fatal with some species.

Stonefish
This brown-grey, lumpy fish inhabits tropical waters of the Pacific and south Asia. Its coloration makes its very hard to spot on the sea floor when walking, and it has potentially lethal venom in its dorsal fins.

Toadfishes
A small, grey fish of only 3–4in (7–10cm) that lives in tropical South American waters. It buries itself in coastal sands, its highly venomous back spines pointing upwards.

sand to protect themselves from predators, and leave a small ventilation hole at the top of the shaft. Sprinkling salt around this hole will bring the animal to the surface; otherwise, simply hook it out with a piece of wire or a stick. Shellfish are responsible for some of the worst forms of food poisoning, however, so they must be cooked thoroughly. Boil or steam them for at least five minutes, preferably within an hour of being caught. Healthy mussels should open their shells after cooking – discard any that stay closed.

Of all the shellfish, crabs offer one of the most substantial meals. Crabs are found along most rocky coastlines around the world. Check rock pools and under seaweed, both places where crabs shelter and feed. They are easily picked up, but watch out for the powerful claws. Kill and cook the crab by plunging it into a large pot of boiling water. Next, twist off the legs and claws and put them to one side (do not throw them away as they contain edible meat). Insert a sharp knife between the two halves of the main shell and twist the knife to prise them apart. With the innards of the crab exposed, cut away the stomach and the two gills, and scrape away any green matter. Once these poisonous parts have been removed, the white meat can be extracted.

FISHING

Fish remain the most important food to be found in water. There are about 25,000 different species, but almost all fall into one of two categories: saltwater fish and freshwater fish.

Freshwater fish

Freshwater fish inhabit inland rivers, streams and non-tidal lakes, though some will live in the freshwater stretches of estuaries. The advantage of freshwater fish for the survival fisherman is that they tend to live in the shallower waters around the banks, and can be fished without leaving the safety of solid land. Species of freshwater fish that pack large amounts of edible meat include: bream, trout, carp, tench, rudd, pike, perch, walleye and pickerel.

Saltwater fish

Saltwater fish inhabit the world's seas and oceans, and saltwater rivers and lakes. Unlike freshwater fish, saltwater fish are more likely to be caught from a boat positioned over deep water, though many types do swim close enough to the coastlines to be caught by angling or netting.

All fishing begins with knowing where to look for the fish. In the seas and oceans, this is relatively easy, as casting a line into any section of deep water is likely to attract some type of fish. Swarms of seabirds attacking patches of water can indicate shoals of fish just beneath the surface, as can a heavy presence of seals, dolphins or sharks. In inland waterways, fish are attracted to places where they can rest and feed without feeling threatened by predators. Shaded places are preferred, such as those under overhanging trees, banks and rocks. Fish will also take rest in the still waters immediately downstream of objects such as large rocks or gravel banks, which break the flow of the current. In fast-flowing water, the insides of bends have a slower current than the outside, and so are another ideal resting places for fish. Most freshwater fish enjoy sunlight, and in colder weather they tend to head for sunny, shallow patches at the edge of the water. A more direct sign that fish are present is bubbles and ripples on the water's surface. These usually suggest that a fish is feeding or snatching at water-skimming insects.

ANGLING

At its most basic, angling requires a hook, line and rod, with floats, weights and lures as

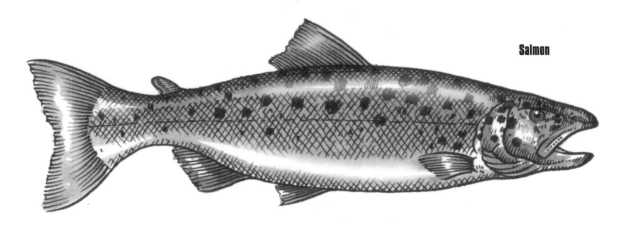

Salmon

175

Barracuda

recommended additions. In survival circumstances, all these can be manufactured from natural materials, and a survival fishing rod can be nothing more than a long stick with some string attached. Commercial line, however, will perform far better than line improvised out of natural grasses and plant fibres. Two rolls of line take up almost no space and should always be carried on any outdoor adventure.

Improvised fish hooks are made out of thorns, nails or pins, even shards of wood. Nails and pins are simply bent into a hook shape, whereas a thorn hook takes some manufacturing. Wooden hooks are less effective than thorn hooks but can be used in an emergency. Simply tie a thin, straight shard of wood to the end of the line and wrap it with bait. The shard should initially be in line with the fishing line. This makes it easy for the fish to swallow, but it will then turn and snag in the fish's mouth.

Whatever hook is used, its performance is improved by using floats, weights and bait. Floats help you to see when a fish is biting on the hook, and also control the depth of water that the hook descends to. Any buoyant material, such as a cork or small piece of wood, will act as a float. Rose-hips are even better because they are easily threaded onto line and their bright red colour is highly visible from the bank.

The distance set between the float and the hook should, technically, be the depth to which the hook descends. However, hooks that are too light (which is particularly the case with thorn hooks) are easily carried to the surface by the currents, and so need weighting to sink back down. The best weights are the purpose-designed split shot used by fishermen, which are simply slipped onto the line near the hook. If these are not available, small stones, buttons, pieces of metal or any other minor weight will suffice. Weights can be placed below the hook on a extended piece of line, a configuration that gives a very deep hook position that is less susceptible to surface currents.

Bait is anything that attracts a fish to the hook, and there is a surprisingly broad range of bait. Living bait includes the traditional fisherman's stock of worms, mussels and maggots. These types of bait have the advantage of moving underwater, which makes them more likely to be spotted by a fish and mistaken for an easy meal. Any large winged insect will also attract fish. Some inanimate objects make effective baits and lures. Attaching a small feather to a hook will attract curious fish, especially if the feather is slapped on the surface of the water a few times to imitate a skimming insect. Shiny objects such as pieces of tin foil and metal will have a similar effect. Almost any piece of

Making fishing hooks

Find a thorny bush, such as a bramble hedge, and cut out a section of stem about 1in (2.5cm) long that has a large thorn at one end (A). At the thornless end, cut a notch around the circumference (B). Tie the fishing line into this notch to stop the hook slip-

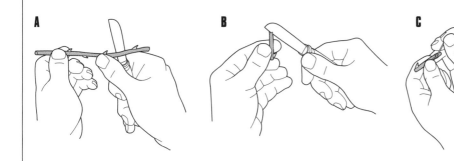

ping off when a fish bites (C–F). The strength of a thorn hook will depend on factors such as the state of the plant material and the size of the fish, but remember that the hook might need replacing after a couple of hours of softening in the water.

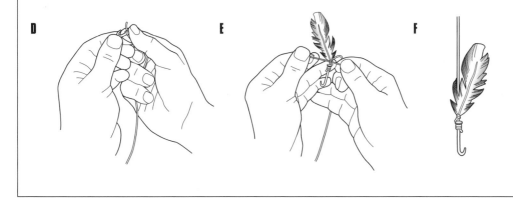

food can serve as bait. The best kinds are those eaten by local fish, such as berries that overhang a river or insects common to the area. Raw meat, fruit, vegetables, bread, cheese and peanuts are attractive baits for many scavenging fish. Try out many different bait varieties until you find one that works.

Professional angling is a technically demanding sport, but its survival equivalent is far more straightforward. For rod fishing,

cast your line out into the water to a position where fish might be. Catching the fish is likely to be a long process, so prop up the rod on the bank using a v-shaped stick stuck in the ground. Position yourself so that the fish cannot see you. Because water refracts light, the fish's field of vision over the bank edge is often wider than your vision into the water. For this reason, keep low down when sitting at the water's edge. Don't let your shadow

Correct use of float and line

In this configuration, the bait is simply attached to the float via a short length of line. The bait will be circulated more around the surface of the water by the currents and so is a good method of catching fish which attack surface insects.

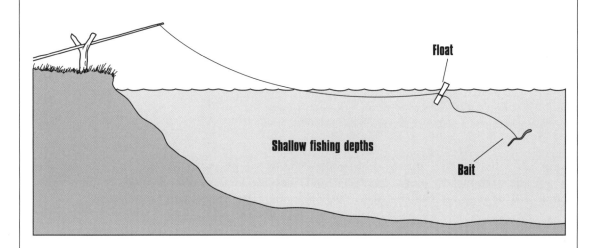

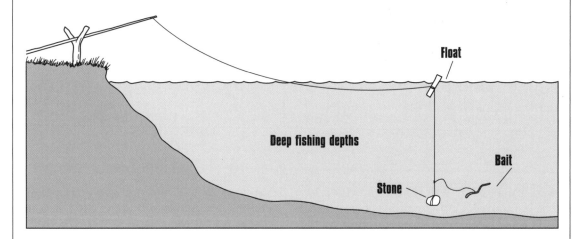

This method is used when attempting to catch fish which swim near the river or sea bed. A small stone hangs from the float on a piece of line. The hook and bait are attached to this by an additional piece of line. The weight of the stone stops the bait from being drawn upwards towards the surface remaining in the fish's habitat.

fall on the water, as it will alert the fish to your presence.

Rather than sitting for long periods watching a line, setting up a nightline is more profitable in terms of the catch and your time. Take a long section of line and attach hooks at regular intervals along its length. Then, tie one end of the line to a fixed object on the bank, and the other to a weight. Cast the weight into the water as far as the line will allow and let it to sink to the bottom. The nightline fishes the full depth of the water and affords multiple opportunities for catching fish. Leave it out for the entire night and in the morning draw it in to check for fish. Remember to change the bait regu-

larly and do not leave the line out past daybreak, or predators will steal your catch.

Spearing

Spearing brings to fishing the world of hunting. Stealth, speed and a strong weapon are required. Because water is so much denser than air, stone-throwing projectile weapons are not suitable for fishing, as the stone loses almost all its force and direction when it enters the water. Guns can be used, but shooting at fish usually consumes large amounts of ammunition. There is also the danger that the end of the barrel might enter the water. When the barrel is underwater, the pressure of detonation is actually blown

Constructing a running line

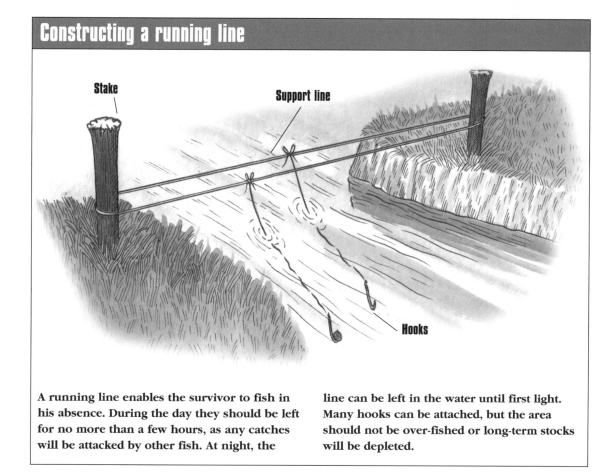

A running line enables the survivor to fish in his absence. During the day they should be left for no more than a few hours, as any catches will be attacked by other fish. At night, the line can be left in the water until first light. Many hooks can be attached, but the area should not be over-fished or long-term stocks will be depleted.

backwards, and the barrel is likely to explode with potentially lethal consequences. If hunting fish with a gun, therefore, only shoot from a safe position on the bank.

Spearing fish is standard practice amongst many coastal and river communities throughout the tropical world. A simple harpoon begins with a long, straight stick about 5-6ft (1.6-2m) long, trimmed of all branches and irregularities. Sharpen one end of the stick and pass the point through the flames of a fire to harden it. This is the most basic harpoon, and the least effective. Harpoons with multiple spikes instead of a single point are better because they increase the striking area. To make a spiked harpoon, tie several sharp thorns or sharpened sticks to the end of the spear. The spikes will be held more securely if they are seated in pre-carved slots and notches. Splay the spikes outward in several directions by lodging a small piece of wood between them. An arrow can be similarly adjusted to make the bow and arrow an additional fishing tool.

Spearing fish usually requires entering the water. Walk slowly and silently, without splashing or causing excessive rippling. Don't move with your shadow in front of you, because it will alert the fish that you are coming. Position yourself directly over the fish, for the shallower the angle, the more refraction will confuse your aim. Allow for refraction in any circumstances by aiming the spear at a point slightly lower than the fish appears. Thrust the spear swiftly into the water and skewer the fish. As soon as you have speared the fish, leave the water. Predators will be attracted to your kill by the smell of blood and the distressed animal's struggles.

Trapping fish

In survival circumstances, fish traps generally produce better results than angling or spearing (the exception being the nightline). Fish traps and nets may take time to construct, but once set up, they will work for as long as they are left in the water, leaving you free to do other things.

Using a spiked harpoon

Spiked harpoons are simple to construct from a branch, twine and several sharp, sturdy thorns. Any spear should have a long length of string attached to the end so that it is easily retrieved if dropped or thrown into the water. When not in use, stick a cork or wedge of leaves on the spikes to protect them from damage.

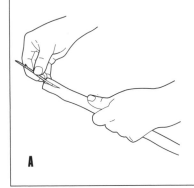

A

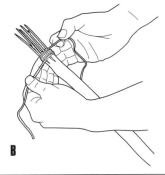

B

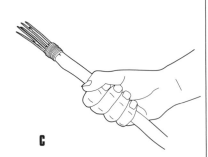

C

Fish tickling

Fish tickling is an ancient fishing method that is now illegal in most countries. The only place where it remains an approved, and much used, way of catching fish is the Falkland islands. To 'tickle' a fish, stand over it in the water, or kneel over it from the bank. Slide your hands very smoothly, slowly and gently into the water and cup them beneath the fish. Then, in a lightning-fast action, scoop the fish onto the bank, where it can be retrieved. Alternatively, grasp the fish firmly in both hands, bending it at the waist and drawing it hard into your stomach. This grip will stop the fish struggling and slipping away. It can be very difficult to tickle fish in open water, but building an enclosure trap will make the process easier. In tidal rivers and estuaries, construct a semicircular wall against the riverbank that is lower than the water level at high tide, but higher than the water level at low tide. When the tide recedes, fish will remain trapped in the enclosure, and are easier to pursue for tickling, netting and spearing.

Bottle traps and basket traps

The most basic fish trap is the bottle trap. This requires nothing more than a plastic bottle. Cut the neck off the bottle, invert it and then wedge it back inside the base. The trap works when a fish swims through the inverted neck of the bottle to reach bait placed inside the base. While the trap is easy for the fish to swim into, it is difficult for it to swim back out through the narrow spout. The fish remains trapped in the base, ready for you to collect. A similar trap can be made out of saplings. Bind the saplings together in a dense pattern to form a hollow torpedo

How to use a bottle trap

The bottle trap is a tried and tested method of fish trapping, and simple to execute in a survival situation. Site the trap in places where fish are likely to gather, such as under the shade of a tree overhanging the water. If placing the bottle in areas of strong currents be sure to weight it down with rocks to stop it being swept away.

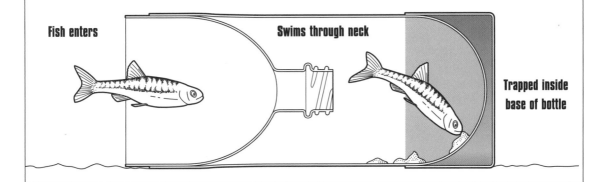

Fish enters   **Swims through neck**   **Trapped inside base of bottle**

shape (to brace the 'wall' of the torpedo outwards, bend and tie very flexible twigs into circular shapes). One end of the torpedo is tied shut, while the other features an opening made from a funnel of twigs inverted into the trap in the same way as the bottle trap. The whole structure is covered with twine to stop a fish escaping through the sides.

One way to make bottle and basket traps more effective is to direct the flow of a river or stream into their mouths. Do this by building up two rock walls in a funnel shape in the water, with the wide part of the funnel facing into the flow of the current. Place the entrance of the trap you are using against the narrow exit of the funnel. The rock funnel channels fish straight into your trap as they swim with the current.

One-way traps

One-way traps can be used on creatures apart from fish. A crab cage is made from sticks tied together in a box structure. One end of the trap is hinged to make a door that only opens inwards – a stick braced across the side of the door stops it opening outwards. Bait the trap and place it in rocky areas of coastal shallows. Crabs and lobsters will push open the trap door to get at the bait, but are trapped when the door closes behind them.

Using a basket trap

Basket traps are most effective in places where fish are swept through a confined space into the basket mouth. A channel can be made using rocks to funnel the fish into the trap, but this results in very intensive catches so the trap must be checked regularly to stop it over filling.

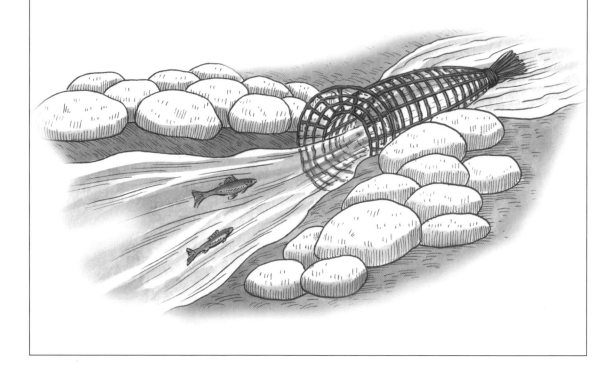

Nets

While traps will catch small numbers of fish, nets are the best way of getting large amounts in one go. A gill net is laborious to make, but the effort is worthwhile for it can trap entire shoals of fish. First, tie two pieces of rope between two trees, parallel to each other and with a space of about 4ft (1.2

Damming

Partially damming a river with a log construction creates a narrow outflow to one side. This is netted to catch fish being swept along by the increased speed of current. Exercise caution when collecting the fish from the net, as the outflow can be very fast flowing. Use a long pole as a brace on the river bed when entering the water, or draw the net in from the bank.

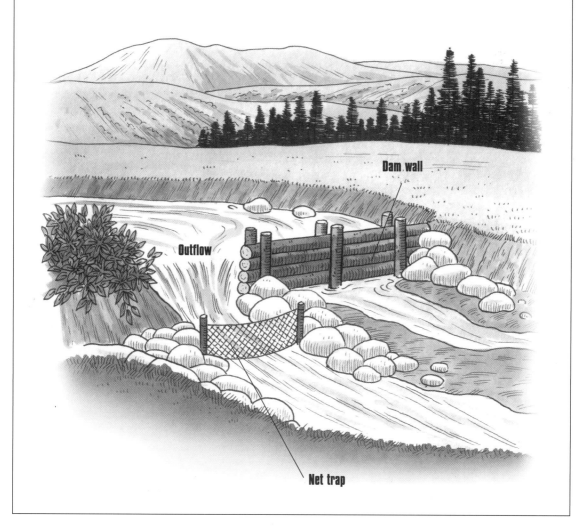

Dam wall

Outflow

Net trap

metres) between them. Then, start attaching other pieces of rope vertically and horizontally between the two main ropes to form a net. The mesh size should be about 4cm (1.5in) and where all the ropes intersect, they must be knotted together.

Gill nets

A simple way to use gill nets is to cast them into water and haul them back in with their catch. This is the least productive method, however. A better alternative is to stretch the net across the width of an entire river by staking the top rope of the net securely between the banks, and weighting the bottom rope so that it sinks to the river floor. Placing the gill net at a 45° angle across the current will prevent most driftwood and vegetation becoming snared in the net and damaging it. Using the gill net across a river results in huge catches in very short spaces of time. Do not apply this method for too long (about an hour will usually do) or too often, as it will decimate a local fish population and leave you with no long-term reserves.

Another, less excessive, way to channel fish into your gill net (or any trap) is by partially damming the river. Pick a bend where the river widens and the current slows down. Across one half of the river, build up a wall of rocks and logs several feet/metres higher than the surface of the water. Across the other half of the river, stretch the gill net, supported between two wooden posts driven into the riverbed. The effect of the dam is to divert fish into the outflow by its side, and straight into the net.

Purse seining

Gill nets have another application called 'purse seining'. This involves two people and is used to bring in entire shoals of fish from shallow waters. Each person takes one end of the net. One person stays on the shore, however, while the other takes the net on his shoulder and walks as far out as possible into the water. The offshore person then lowers his net into the water and walks back to the shoreline, taking a long curving route. As he does so, the net forms a large semicircular 'purse', which traps fish between the net and shore. All it then takes is for both people to drag the net up onto the beach, where the fish are collected and killed. This technique can be successfully performed at night, with the addition of torches or firebrands. At night,

Safety when fishing

Follow these simple precautions to avoid accidents while fishing:

- If possible, wear gloves when handling fish as protection from sharp fins and teeth.
- When using offal at sea to attract fish, do not put your hands into the water to land fish. Predators may confuse them with the bait.
- Do not touch fishing line with your bare hands when reeling in.
- Never wrap fishing line around your hands for a stronger grip.
- When venturing into fast currents, use a long stick dug into the riverbed and held upstream for a more stable stance.
- Beware of underwater hazards such as rocks and weeds. If the water level rises at one point, it suggests a rock beneath.
- Work out how you are going to land large fish before you set about catching them.
- Never jump or dive into water.

Avoiding fish's line of sight

The refraction of light through water gives a fish a broad angle of vision over a river bank. A fisherman should keep as low to the ground as possible when approaching the bank to stay under the fish's line of sight. He should also keep his shadow from falling on the water and alerting the fish to his presence.

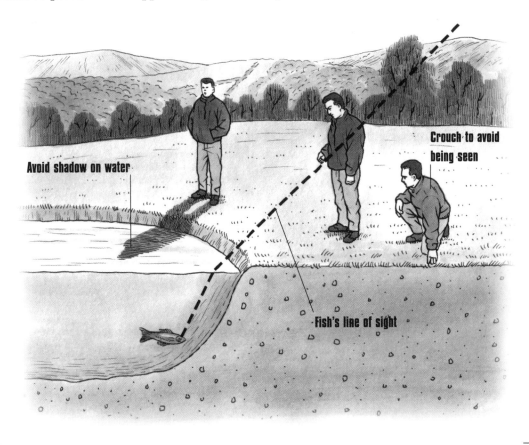

Avoid shadow on water

Crouch to avoid being seen

Fish's line of sight

fish are attracted to bright lights, so the torches can lure more of them into the 'purse' before it is closed. Catching fish with gill nets frequently provides the survivor with more fish than he actually needs. Oversupplies of fish are a problem because, in hot climates, any meat that cannot be eaten or preserved in hours will go off and become a health hazard. A less powerful alternative to the gill net, therefore, is a dip net.

Dip nets

Dip nets are handheld nets much like the ones used by children in seaside resorts. They can be made out of any water-permeable piece of fabric – cotton t-shirts are particularly convenient. Find a thin sapling and cut off a long forked section. Feed the forks of the sapling into the hem of the t-shirt until they touch at the midpoint. Make a nick in the fabric at this point, pull the sapling ends

Distilling seawater

Desalinating seawater is usually performed by boiling the water and channelling the steam through a pipe into a cooler container, where the steam condenses into fresh water. The salt content and any impurities are left behind as a residue. Whether using a board (A) or a leaf (B) to seal the boiling vessel, the seal must be as tight as possible to stop the escape of steam.

through and tie them firmly. Making a knot in the sleeve end of the t-shirt will complete the net.

This type of net is not a sophisticated fishing device but it is a practical one. To use it, walk slowly into a river or stream and then kick up clouds of mud from the riverbed. The mud swirling through the water reduces the levels of oxygen available to the fish. To find more oxygen, they swim to the surface, where they can be directed into the dip net. Lift the net slowly from the water with the fish inside, then nip the opening together to prevent the fish from leaping over the side back into the river.

Baiting a dip net may attract many different varieties of fish. To attract eels, place a quantity of fish offal or animal dung mixed with straw or bracken at the bottom of the net. The eels are attracted to the bait and will accidentally knot themselves into the straw while feeding. If left overnight, the net should contain several eels by the morning.

FINDING WATER AT SEA

Freshwater environments offer much to aid the survivor. Drinking water and fish are in abundance. The water stimulates the growth of many types of edible plants along the bank. Land animals come to the water to drink, where they can be hunted or trapped.

The sea is less forgiving. Fish are obviously plentiful, but fresh drinking water is not. Despite being surrounded by water, the survivor at sea is effectively in a desert if he cannot find fresh water or convert seawater into fresh water. Those lost at sea in life-rafts are also exposed to a number of factors that cause dehydration. While the sun encourages sweating, the salt spray from the sea will simultaneously dry out the skin and speed up fluid loss.

Most modern life-rafts come complete with supplies of drinking water, solar stills and chemical desalination kits. However, survival equipment frequently goes missing from life-rafts on many boats, and finding containers of water can never abe guaranteed. Even if these items are present, it's best to gather as much water as possible using other techniques, should the technology run out or fail.

Drinking seawater and urine are never options when surviving at sea, and alcohol and smoking must be avoided. Remember not to eat if water supplies are especially low. Fish and seaweed in particular use large amounts of water during digestion.

Rain is the most important source of freshwater at sea. As soon as a downpour looks likely, set up as many open containers as possible to collect the water. Stand buckets and bottles on the decks, but steady them with heavy objects to stop them falling over and spilling valuable fluids. If there are puddles of freshwater on the floor of the boat that cannot be transferred to containers, drink these first before they evaporate.

The only ways to turn seawater into fresh water are through desalination chemicals, a solar still or by distillation. Desalination chemicals come with instructions on usage – usually a simple matter of dropping tablets into a container of seawater. Solar stills used to extract freshwater from seawater differ from those used on land environments. To make a solar still for sea use, fill a large bowl with a few inches of seawater, and set an empty container in the middle. Do not allow any of the saltwater to slop over into the container. Now stretch a plastic sheet over the edge of the bowl and weight it in the middle so that the centre of the sheet hangs down over the container inside. Make sure that seal between the plastic and the bowl is airtight.

Place the entire machine out in the sun. As the seawater evaporates in the heat, it leaves the salt particles behind because they are too heavy to be suspended in the air. The water vapour condenses against the plastic and runs down into the container. Once all the seawater has evaporated, the container should provide a drink of clean, freshwater.

Distillation kits work on a similar principle to solar stills, but they also need fire to work. Making fire is not always possible or advisable on a boat, but some life-rafts will contain small cooking stoves for emergencies. Distillation requires two vessels. One is filled with seawater and covered over tightly, except for a tube inserted into the top of the container. This tube should not touch the water inside. The other end of the tube goes into an empty container, similarly sealed. When a fire is made under the pot containing the seawater, the salt-free steam travels along the tube and exits into the cold container. Because of the temperature difference between the steam and the container, the steam condenses into water. Placing the receptacle in a container of cold water to reduce the internal air temperature will speed up the cooling of the steam. The virtue of the distillation method is that you can make freshwater on demand as long as a heat source is available.

Glossary

activated charcoal – charcoal which has been treated to increase its ability to absorb fluids.

amino acid – an organic compound which occurs naturally in plant and animal tissues and which is a basic constituent of proteins.

amphibians – a cold-blooded class of animals which have an aquatic larval stage (gill breathing) and a land-dwelling adult stage (lung breathing).

anaphylactic shock – a severe allergic reaction which can result in massive swelling and respiratory and circulatory distress/failure.

antibody – a blood protein which attacks bacteria, viruses and other foreign substances which enter the human blood.

bird lime – a glutinous substance spread onto branches to trap birds.

bola missile – a weapon consisting of multiple weights bound together by rope and thrown to bring down prey.

bore – the internal diameter of a gun barrel.

calorie – the energy needed to heat 1 gram of water through 1°C.

carbohydrate – an organic compound of carbon, hydrogen and oxygen found in many foods. When ingested they are broken down to provide energy.

carotid arteries – the two main arteries which supply blood to the head and neck.

chlorine – a chemical element which, amongst other purposes, is added to water as a purifying agent.

cholesterol – an organic compound found in human blood, nerves and cells, an excess of which can lead to atherosclerosis.

combination guns – a firearm which features a rifled barrel and a smooth-bore barrel for firing bullets and shot respectively.

coniferous – denotes an evergreen tree with cones and needle-like leaves.

deadfall trap – a trap designed to kill an animal by dropping a heavy weight on it.

deciduous – a tree which sheds its leaves annually.

dehydration – in a person, a significant loss of body fluids which is not replaced by fluid intake.

dysentery – a chronic diarrhoeal illness which can lead to severe dehydration and death.

endotherm – an animal which produces its own heat internally, as in the case of humans.

evapotranspiration – the process of water being transferred from the land to the atmosphere via evaporation.

fats – natural oily substances which, in humans, are derived from food and deposited in subcutaneous layers and around some major organs.

fibre – a constituent of some foods which

resists the process of breakdown by the digestive system.

grains – a unit of weight which is approximately 0.0648 grams.

heat exhaustion – a medical condition in which the body's core temperature rises above its normal range of 36-38°C (97.8-100.4°F).

hydrocyanic acid – a poisonous solution of hydrogen cyanide in water, found in some plants.

iodine – a chemical element which has a use in water purification.

jugular vein – one of several large veins which transport blood to the head and face.

kindling – small pieces of dry material, usually thin twigs, which are added to ignited tinder to develop a fire.

lure – anything used in fishing or hunting which tempts prey into a trap or particular location.

mammals – warm-blooded vertebrates which usually give birth to live young.

minerals – inorganic substances which the human body requires to maintain health.

monsoon – a period of intense rainfall and wind in India and southeast Asia between May and September annually.

oxalic acid – a poisonous acid present in plants such as wood sorrel, rhubarb leaves and others.

pemmican – a durable food made from a mix of dried meat and animal fat.

photosynthesis – the process by which green plants produce food from carbon dioxide and water using sunlight.

plankton – microscopic creatures which float in vast quantities around the world's oceans and seas.

potassium permanganate – a chemical which can be used to sterilise water.

proteins – organic compounds which form an essential part of living organisms. Amongst other things, they are integral to the function of body tissue, muscle and antibodies.

prussic acid – another term for hydrocyanic acid.

purse seining – a fishing net or seine which is formed into the shape of a bag and used to draw shoals of fish into shore.

rabbit starvation – a state of de facto starvation resulting from a diet exclusively of rabbits, these taking more nutritional elements from the human body during digestion than they actually provide.

rainforest – a forest growth in tropical areas characterised by heavy annual rainfall and a massive proliferation of plant and animal life.

savannah – grassy plains of tropical and subtropical regions with flat terrain and very few trees.

scurvy – a potentially fatal illness caused by a lack of vitamin C in the diet.

sign – a term used in tracking for any disturbances in the natural environment which indicate the passage of quarry.

solar still – a device which traps moisture from the earth under a plastic sheet, this condensing out into drinkable water.

temperate – any climate which is characterised by mild temperatures.

tinder – small pieces of light and dry material which are very easily ignited and are used to initiate a fire.

transpiration bag – a plastic bag tied around vegetation to trap water vapour emitted by the plant and condense it out into drinking water.

tropical – denotes the latitudes 23° 26′ north or south of the equator.

tularaemia – a potentially fatal bacterial disease passed from animals to humans which results in fever, weight loss and ulcers.

vitamins – a group of organic compounds which are an essential part of human nutrition, though are only required in very small doses.

watertable – the level in the ground below which the soil is saturated with water.

Index